THE KILLING SEASON

THE KILLING SEASON

MEMOIRS OF A MERCENARY IN THE CONGO 1965–1967

TERRY NORMAN

Pen & Sword
MILITARY
AN IMPRINT OF PEN & SWORD BOOKS LTD.
YORKSHIRE – PHILADELPHIA

First published in Great Britain in 2025 by
PEN AND SWORD MILITARY
An imprint of
Pen & Sword Books Limited
Yorkshire – Philadelphia

ISBN 978 1 03612 561 5

A CIP catalogue record for this book is available from the British Library.

Typeset in Times New Roman 11.5/14 by
SJmagic DESIGN SERVICES, India.
Printed and bound in the UK by CPI Group (UK) Ltd.

The Publisher's authorised representative in the EU for product safety is Authorised Rep Compliance Ltd., Ground Floor, 71 Lower Baggot Street, Dublin D02 P593, Ireland.
www.arccompliance.com

For a complete list of Pen & Sword titles please contact
PEN & SWORD BOOKS LIMITED
George House, Units 12 & 13, Beevor Street, Off Pontefract Road,
Barnsley, South Yorkshire, S71 1HN, England
E-mail: enquiries@pen-and-sword.co.uk
Website: www.pen-and-sword.co.uk

or

PEN AND SWORD BOOKS
1950 Lawrence Rd, Havertown, PA 19083, USA
E-mail: uspen-and-sword@casematepublishers.com
Website: www.penandswordbooks.com

FSC www.fsc.org
MIX
Paper | Supporting responsible forestry
FSC® C013604

CONTENT

FOREWORD

Due to outside pressure and inside liberal ideals of the then Belgian Government, that vast landmass on the African continent, known simply to the man in the street as Congo, was granted independence on 30 June 1960. Since that date, for the rest of the decade, the Congo strode the world headlines with awful precision. Public interest being created by the country's interior politics, wars, assassinations, atrocities, public hangings and international debts – all amounting to a terrifying breakdown in law and order. So much so that the United Nations Organisation, a principal force behind the Congo gaining self-government, began to eye its monster child with obvious annoyance.

However, in the knowledge that the Congo was too big to hide and too strategically placed in Africa to ignore, certain world powers sought to establish the Congo in the communist camp while other world powers, notably the United States of America and Belgium, were actively engaged in trying to keep it orientated towards the West. A task which was frustrating, thankless and, at times, downright embarrassing.

This book is about the Congo of the mid-sixties. Except for President Mobutu and the late Patrice Lumumba, all the names mentioned herein are fictitious, although many of the incidents are drawn from life. Indeed, it could not be otherwise as the Congo of the sixties left very little to the imagination. In the cause of 'African solidarity and nationalism' many place names were changed in June 1966, but as this book covers the period before and just after this date the original names e.g. Leopoldville (now Kinshasa) remain unaltered.

'Op-Sud', the Government nerve centre in the war against the Armee Populaire de Liberation, existed. So did the American military advisers; the CIA men; the Free Cuban pilots; the 'Makasi' boys who serviced their aircraft; the mercenaries – they all existed and probably some are still there. Like Red China's military and political advisers based in Tanzania; the Cuban guerilla war specialists loyal to Castro, not forgetting the communist instructors safe in Bulgaria, East Germany and the Soviet Union.

Sponsorship by interested external powers – political, physical and monetary – will always be there to some degree. It is in many other African states, because the geographical value and the mineral wealth of that great continent have yet to be fully explored and exploited.

'You cannot separate the just from the unjust and the good from the wicked;
For they stand together before the face of the sun even as the black thread and the white are woven together.
And when the black thread breaks, the weaver shall look into the whole cloth, and he shall examine the loom also.'

KAHLIL GIBRAN
The Prophet

CHAPTER ONE

There was little he could do about his impending fate.

He had jumped – leapt from the truck and all too late, he glimpsed the rebel aiming at him from the tall grass. A spasm of terror clutched his throat, the taste of copper filled his mouth as the rebel fired. The bullet flicked through his flapping khaki shirt, burned across his right ribs, and buried itself in the truck behind him. Morgan instinctively rushed forward and brought his rifle barrel down on to his adversary's head. He fired a short burst at point-blank range as the rebel toppled sideways and then he dived for cover.

Shooting was continuous on either side of him. The convoy had certainly run into a right ambush this time, he thought, expending a quick succession of rounds at the shadowy figures in the dense bush.

Morgan's fellow mercenaries were in similar situations and, knowing what end awaited them if captured, they laid down a curtain of fire into the bush on both sides of the narrow road. Any panic was channelled through the barrels of their Belgian FN rifles. The smattering of Congolese troops in the same convoy wildly joined in the shooting in a bid to save their own skins.

True to the old war maxim of minutes of fear, seconds of sheer terror, the firing intensified before petering out altogether at the repeated shouts of Machine-g John Vivian, a South African like Morgan himself. The rebels, supporters of the late Patrice Lumumba, had departed from the scene. A quick check among the mercenary commando column indicated two men killed and two wounded, one of the wounded being an ANC man.

The rebels had suffered more as a hasty body-count showed, but the final figure would have to be pure conjecture. Certainly, blood trails leading into the bush indicated other hits, but there could be no follow through. Time was of the essence.

The wounded men were made as comfortable as possible while the two mercenary dead were wrapped in groundsheets and lifted on to the end truck. The remaining thirty-eight mercenaries with the twenty-four ANC personnel reloaded their weapons and took their places in the convoy again. The motorised column, comprising seven battered trucks and headed by two jeeps with yellow identification panels over their bonnets, moved on. Everyone on board was grateful in no small way to the poor marksmanship on the rebels' part.

'That little thrash should have finished us,' said Vivian after he lit two cigarettes, passing one to his driver. 'Too bloody close that time.'

An English mercenary on Morgan's truck cocked his rifle when he saw a bend in the road ahead of the convoy.

'Two ambushes in one day and the fourth in a week,' he shouted above the whine of the truck's engine. 'Is it really worth it, Roy?'

'Well, something must be worth this fighting, but don't ask me what,' replied Morgan, also keeping two vigilant eyes on the fast-approaching bend.

'Don't fret about it,' interjected a mercenary named Kemble who spoke with a strong Australian accent. 'Just think of the money.'

'I do, but I haven't heard a dicky bird whether any has gone into my bank account yet,' grumbled the Englishman.

'Jesus!' exclaimed Kemble. 'Do you expect to get a letter of confirmation when you're stuck out in the middle of nowhere? Jesus,' said Kemble again to Morgan, 'I'm sure this guy thinks he's on his daddy's yacht.'

The ominous bend came and went. The convoy rolled along the narrow dirt road with the sun sinking fast on their right flank.

Vivian decided that the moment had arrived to camp for the night. Sentries were posted and the two dead men, one English and one German, were consigned to shallow graves. The mercenary machine-g presided over the brief burial ceremony.

'First-class men,' he said after reciting the Lord's Prayer from memory with all the religious zeal of a dawn hangover in a Brothel. He turned to a sergeant on his right. 'Cover them over, Sergeant Davis.'

Davis issued the necessary order, and earth was shovelled back into the rectangular holes. A buddy of the dead English mercenary knocked up a crude cross and hammered it in at the head of the Englishman's grave. Someone suggested that the German's eternal resting place should have some mark of identification before the actual grave disappeared back into the African landscape. It was mutually agreed to remove the breech lock from the German mercenary's rifle and put his helmet over the butt. After all, the helmet he had worn so assiduously up to his sudden demise might as well serve him usefully now that he was dead, since it hardly helped him when he was alive. The German's FN rifle was duly stuck into the earth and the helmet with the fatal bullet hole just above the rim was dropped on top.

The rest of the evening and night passed without incident and, at first light, the mercenaries broke camp. Their destination, Paulis.

They stopped at noon to rest and to eat. The operator in the signals truck tuned into the air frequency of the friendly B26 passing overhead. The aircraft transmitted a message which made the operator swear nervously. He rushed the message to Vivian.

'We've got trouble, sir. There's a body of Simbas, approximate strength of six-hundred, at this map reference.' He jabbed a finger on to the map he held. 'Our instructions from Sunray is to rescue and evacuate any white civilians still in the area.'

'Oh, Christ!' exclaimed Vivian. 'What about, our final destination?' He looked up at the circling B26. 'Signal back and ask him for clarification of our main objective.'

The operator climbed into his signals truck and made contact again. Vivian stood impatiently by the tailboard, fingering his moustache. 'Roger and out,' concluded the operator. He glanced at Vivian. 'Civilians come first.'

'Bloody hell,' said Vivian in frustration. 'Where's the fucking loot in civilians? It's towns we need. Towns like Paulis.'

Machine-g Vivian studied his map of the surrounding area. The column's sergeant medic, a Scotsman from Kilmarnock, approached him. 'The wounded are in a bad way, sir, particularly Volunteer Cromby. Internal bleeding.'

The mercenary officer rubbed his jaw in troubled thought.

'Okay, Sergeant,' he said at length. 'Put them in the one-tonner and try to give them a steady ride as best you can. The one-tonner can bring up the end of the column. It's about the safest place if I have to give the order to attack. Hopefully, you'll be able to avoid using cowboy tactics. Leave such things to the rest of us.'

The convoy moved on. Four hours later, negotiating some difficult stretches where jungle overhung the road, the mercenaries came to a spot which had little vegetation. It was there they made camp. Early next morning they continued to the map reference given to them by the B26 pilot. It was the usual plantation layout and very shortly a single-storey house with outbuildings came into view. They could not really miss it as most of the outbuildings were in flames. Vivian led the convoy direct to the house with a sinking heart. The rebels appeared to have won the race. He hopped from his jeep and ran up the steps to the house. It opened before him, and standing in the doorway, was a grizzled old white planter clasping a .375 Cogswell & Harrison sporting rifle. The old man spoke to Vivian in French. Vivian's schoolboy French was just not up to the job. 'Parlez vous Anglais?' he asked, feeling slightly stupid.

'Yes,' replied the old man heavily. 'I speak some English.'

'You the only one here?'

The planter shook his head. 'There's two Greeks in the first room. They were traders until the uprising overtook them a few days ago. They had trouble with their pick-up truck and called into here to see if I had any parts which they could use. The pick-up is around the back. I could not help them.'

Vivian noticed the two Greeks, both middle-aged, appear behind the planter while he talked. They were frightened men, and they brushed passed the planter to speak to Vivian.

'You help us, please you help us,' pleaded one of them.

Vivian nodded reassuringly and turned to Davis who had stepped up to stand beneath the welcome shade of the veranda.

'Take these two and put them in your jeep, Sergeant,' said Vivian. He gazed at the planter, offering him a hand. 'You must come with us. Pack what you can carry with you.'

The old planter's eyes misted over.

'There's nothing I need here, not now,' he said sadly.

Vivian looked over his shoulder and into a room full of furniture and personal possessions which had obviously been lovingly acquired over the years. 'Are you sure?'

He watched the old man shake his head dejectedly.

'How can I take a lifetime of hope and endeavour?' He shrugged his shoulders. 'You take what you desire, Machine-g, because the Simbas will strip this place bare. You can rely on it. As for me, nothing. Too many memories.'

Vivian thanked him for the offer and beckoned his driver over. 'Make this gentleman comfortable in the back of my jeep.'

The driver led the old planter away from the house. Vivian glanced again into the room before departing and spied an intricately carved ivory chess set upturned on an occasional table. He swept the pieces into an inlaid box on the same table and slipped home the lid. He picked up the box and the chess board and placed them under his arm. He was fond of chess and a couple of games could pass away any idle time, he surmised.

The mercenary leader retraced his steps to his jeep. 'Do you think there are any more whites in the area?' he asked the planter, who was drinking from his driver's water bottle. The planter wiped his lips.

'I doubt it very much,' he said. 'Except dead ones,' he added.

It was the answer that Vivian hoped would come. He could now proceed to Paulis with a clear conscience. The convoy rolled back to the road. About five miles down the road towards Paulis the column was ambushed.

The ambush was an uncoordinated affair and very spread out. All the same, Vivian had the foresight to judge that it could turn into a very dangerous situation. He sprang from his seat, one hand gripping the stock of his mounted machine gun for balance.

'Move it!' he yelled. 'Move it! Don't stop! For Christ sakes – move it!'

Most of his words were thrown to the wind, but his frantic posturing came through loud and clear. The convoy accelerated in speed and barnstormed down the road. Within a space of five minutes the column had left the ambush behind, or so Vivian thought. The grim realisation struck home when he stopped the convoy to appraise any damage. It was Morgan who gave him the news.

'We've lost the last truck. The one-tonner,' he said.

'What do you mean that we've lost the last truck?' came the blistering response.

'Simply, that,' replied Morgan. 'The boys in the truck in front saw it as we hit the ambush, but it wasn't there when we came out the other side. Everybody was tally-hoing like crazy and nobody looked back.'

'Christ almighty,' breathed Vivian in desperation. 'Well, there's nothing for it, but to go back.'

'All of us?'

'Negative. Just the two jeeps.' He called to Davis who was leaning against the second jeep and in the act of lighting a cigarette, having heard about the missing truck. 'We're going back. You ride shotgun in the other jeep.'

Davis looked aghast. 'Sir,' he exclaimed, 'the poor bastards are probably all dead by now. The wounded were on that truck too, if you remember.'

'Sergeant, of course I bloody remember! But what in the hell gives you the God-given right in telling me that they're all blown away? This jeep and your one is going back. That's final!'

'It probably will be,' grunted Davis as his driver executed a swift three-point turn in the road.

The two jeeps charged back along the road after disembarking the old planter and the two Greeks. Morgan glimpsed Vivian adjusting his black neckerchief to cover his nostrils in an effort to thwart the choking dust that plumed from under the wheels of Davis's jeep.

Roy Morgan checked the time on his watch. It was exactly 14:00 hours. He lit a cigarette. At 14:10 hours the waiting column heard the distant sound of firing. By 14:30 hours both jeeps had rejoined the column. Morgan noticed that Davis's driver was bleeding from a deep gash in his right cheek. The jeep's machine gun hung crookedly from its mounting.

'Some black bastard put a bullet right, into the ammo belt,' fumed Davis. 'The whole bloody works went off. He started taking the machine gun apart. His injured driver tried to speak to him, but every time he opened his mouth, blood would bubble from his punctured cheek and splash over Davis.

'Shove off, man, and find yourself a field dressing,' said Davis intent, on repairing his GPMG. 'You're drowning me in blood.'

Vivian sat despondently in his jeep, staring at Davis wrestling with the machine gun in the other vehicle.

'What do we do now?' asked Morgan.

'Press on to the next village. It's about ten kilometres down the road and the last one before Paulis. We'll camp there and a small force of us will try to retrieve the one-tonner in the morning. We'll be needing that truck before this contract's through, even if the poor sods in it won't be needing us.'

Happily, on their arrival at the village they discovered that the very few people there – all eleven of them – were friendly. The reason was simple, as Vivian found out on closer inspection. They were all lepers. He arranged some food for them before confining them to one hut with strict instructions not to put in an appearance until called upon to do so next morning. Guards were posted around the village and the remainder of the column made themselves comfortable for the night.

Vivian spent a restless night and was glad to see the tropical dawn blossom across the sky. He ordered six men, including Morgan, on to one of the five-ton trucks and, with his jeep in the vanguard, they set off back along the road. Everyone in the two-vehicle convoy kept a weather-eye open for trouble. The small truck that had failed to emerge from the ambush hovered into view.

The area looked deserted, but Vivian decided against any undue risk. He told his driver to stop, simultaneously flagging down the truck behind. He focused his binoculars on the stationary vehicle. He could see that it had veered off the road, just as he had viewed it yesterday before Davis's jeep had come under intensive fire. Vivian swept his binoculars around the periphery of the truck. There were no signs of movement, except for the vultures busying themselves around and on top of the vehicle.

'Any hostile movement?' enquired his driver.

'None so far.' He trained his binoculars on the truck again. 'I can't understand why the rebels didn't set the damn thing alight or something.' Vivian lowered his glasses and turned to the truck behind him. He noted that everyone had their FN rifles at the ready, even the truck driver held a revolver against the rim of his steering wheel. Vivian wished he had brought along the mortar and hoped that the oversight would not have fatal consequences. There were already enough men from his commando who would not see the remaining weeks of 1964.

'We shall halt again midway between this position and the one-tonner,' he called out. 'You blokes on the back of the truck will get down and circle round the one-tonner on this side. We'll advance down the road with covering fire.' He gave them a three-minute start before nudging his driver who was visibly sweating. 'Okay, let's go.'

The jeep lurched forward and stopped. The truck behind almost ran into their rear.

'Sorry, sir,' mumbled the driver. 'I stalled.'

'I can see that,' said Vivian sarcastically. 'Get a grip on yourself, man.'

The pincer-like manoeuvre was completed without a sign of the enemy. Vivian climbed thankfully from his jeep and went to the one-tonner. The vultures had screeched away, frightened off by the gunfire. The truck's windscreen had crazed over, and on closer inspection Vivian saw three bullet holes in it, one of which had passed through the driver's neck. He wrenched open the passenger door and had to side-step hurriedly as the other dead mercenary in the cab tumbled out. The sweet pungent smell coupled with the black, bloated flies buzzing about in the cab interior made him retch. He regained his composure and saw that the cab floor was littered with spent rounds. It was obvious that the rebels did not have it all their own way. The mercenary officer wondered if at least one of the men was still alive on their abortive return to the one-tonner yesterday. It could have accounted for the rebels still being there and the truck just left abandoned.

Roy Morgan and three other mercenaries went to the back of the truck and discovered the remains of the Scottish sergeant medic and the two wounded. All four mercenaries felt sick to the pits of their stomachs. 'Jesus,' said one, averting his eyes.

'Those vultures must have had a field day.'

He registered his disgust by firing at a group of vultures who had flown back to perch in a nearby tree, only to be rebuked by Vivian for wasting precious ammunition. The dead driver and his mate joined the human remnants of the other three men. A young South African ex-motor-mechanic lifted the truck bonnet to inspect the engine for damage. Satisfied that it was in good order, he slammed the bonnet shut, climbed into the cab and turned the ignition switch. The engine whined, then growled into life.

'Well done, Phillips,' shouted Vivian, returning to his jeep. 'You drive it back.'

'Thanks for nothing,' Phillips commented to himself. He found a heavy spanner and smashed out the crazed-over windscreen so that he could see out as well as to let in more air. They arrived back at the village without further incidents.

It was apparent from the state of the bodies that individual graves would be a time-consuming luxury. The objective was to get them into the ground as fast as possible. Sergeant Davis organised a fatigue party from among the ANC contingent and, within an hour, they had dug a substantial pit. The one-tonner was reversed up to the graveside and the two dead mercenaries from the cab, together with the remains of the other three, were shovelled off the back and into the pit. Vivian, trying not to breathe too deeply, said a quick prayer. A token handful of earth was scattered over the dead and a salute fired. The Congolese soldiers under Davis's direction hastily refilled the pit.

Vivian ordered everybody back to the convoy as he made a beeline to the signals truck.

'You know,' said Davis to Morgan as they walked away from the mass grave, 'at this rate, there won't be anyone left to drive into Paulis.'

'It looks that way,' he said. 'All the same, casualties have been fairly light until this week.'

Davis brightened up. 'Yeah, I guess you're right. Let's hope that Paulis has a brewery for us to liberate. It'll take at least a dozen beers to wash the dust and stench out of my system.'

The two mercenaries heard Vivian swearing from inside the signals truck. His voice got louder, and the swearing continued for a full two minutes.

'Has he gone off his head?' muttered Davis.

The mercenary officer jumped from the back of the vehicle, his face a picture of frustration. '56 Commando have beaten us to it,' he growled. 'They're in Paulis right now.'

'Shit!' expressed Davis. 'There won't be a fucking bottle left in the whole damned town. That lot are a bunch of piss artists.'

'Stuff the beer, if there's a worthwhile bank in Paulis they'll have it,' said Morgan 'They've got a top-line explosives expert among their crew, an Afrikaans guy from the Durban Deep mine. A real ace of the base.'

'Shit!' exclaimed Davis for the second time.

They parted company with Davis heading for his jeep. Morgan continued to where his truck was parked in line. He was about to climb aboard when he received word that Vivian wanted to see him. He doubled back to the signals truck.

'We've just had a message from Sunray,' began Vivian gruffly. 'It concerns you and I'm afraid it's bad news.'

'Don't tell me that some admin idiot's mislaid my bank account number,' quipped Morgan.

'Jesus, you will wish it was when I tell you.'

Morgan frowned. 'Hey, it really is bad news?'

Vivian nodded somberly. "You're being repatriated once we get to Paulis." He explained the reason in quiet tones.

Morgan took a deep breath. He gazed along the column of trucks, up to the cloudless sky and then down to the deep brown earth around his combat boots. Everything seemed to merge, then through his mental kaleidoscope he saw Davis stand up in his jeep and light a cigarette. Roy Morgan shook his head, scarcely believing what he had heard. He turned and stared at Vivian.

"oh shit." he echoed

CHAPTER TWO

Paul Lagache, grim-faced and tanned to an unhealthy yellowish colour from a lifetime in the Congo, clutched at the sample of coffee beans from his sixty-six hectometre plantation, situated in the Kivu province on the shores of Lake Tanganyika. He loosened his grip and allowed the bright brown beans to trickle through his fingers into the cupped palm of his left hand, studying each one with an experienced eye.

A tiny vein quivered visibly in his right temple as the last coffee bean dropped down to join the others now nestling in his left hand. Then his hand closed tightly about them until the knuckles formed the profile of the high range of scrub-covered hills in the middle distance. Suddenly, the worries and frustration over the past days welled up inside him. In a sharp burst of temper Lagache flung the bruised beans on to the ground.

He stalked angrily from the coffee bushes to the dirt driveway outside his corrugated iron-roofed bungalow. There, he turned and surveyed the coffee bushes. He ran a trembling hand across his thinning hair.

A year of hard work was in danger of being wasted. The beans would be over-ripe soon and their price would drop drastically on the market. But when would the pickers come? Bad tempered and ill at ease, he strode quickly to his Land Rover, parked in the patchy shade of the palm trees bordering his bungalow.

Slipping his thin body behind the steering wheel, Lagache switched on the engine and shoved the gear lever into first. He cursed the local chief of Kele village as he released the handbrake. He cursed him again when letting the clutch in too quickly, nearly stalling the engine. Clouds of dust spurted behind the rear wheels before the heavy treads gripped the uneven surface. Lagache slammed the gears through to top in quick succession. The trunks of the palm trees lining the plantation track began to blur as he strove for more speed. He stamped briefly on the brake pedal on reaching the corner where the track intersected the road leading to Kele, then he drove even faster – hoping that the torrid breeze flowing past his head would cool his temper before arriving at the village.

It was his second trip to Kele that day and the fourth in the past three days. On those occasions that local chief had neatly evaded Lagache's requests for labour. Knowing intimately the various tribal traditions and superstitions, Lagache was loathe to pursue the point lest the headman take offence. Upon seeing him earlier in the day, however, Lagache suspected that there was more to the villagers seemly lack of cooperation. It was then he turned on Chief Lufundisha – the local chief – and admonished him in bitter terms about his negative attitude.

Now as Lagache travelled to the village, he regretted shouting his mouth off at Chief Lufundisha in front of the villagers. It was a thoroughly stupid move on his part. This time he wouldn't make the same mistake. He would see the chief alone. Then, if logical persuasion failed, he would try bribery to loosen the chief's tongue.

There was also the question concerning his own Congolese staff on the plantation. There was, however, a subtle difference. Whereas the attitude of the villagers was evasive and bordering on the negative, his boys complied with his orders in a hesitant manner. A month back, they went about their tasks with a willing cheerfulness. That cheerfulness was now lacking. Lagache thought he knew why, but he wanted confirmation. Moreover, if his boys behaviour were tied to that of the villagers it was necessary to get to the crux of the matter fast.

Working in his coffee fields was a seasonal event for the villagers. They waited eagerly every year for the beans to ripen, so that for a few weeks in the year they could be fully employed. The extra money would be utilised to purchase new fishing nets, cloth, cheap pots and pans and other requisites from the Indian traders at Lukamba, a small lakeside town eight kilometres due south of Lagache's plantation.

The plantation meant much to him. He'd inherited it from his late father, and, using scientific farming methods, expanded the plantation to the size it was now.

Kele village would never have existed were it not for the Lagache plantation. When his father began clearing the bush the natives of the local Mbembe tribe came to assist him and many stayed to found Kele. When he died in 1953 the work tradition continued under Paul Lagache's direction and authority.

Nothing changed to upset the system, even when the Congo became independent under the late Patrice Lumumba. Lagache thought there might be trouble when Kivu's adjacent provinces, Katanga and southern Kasai, declared their own form of independence. But nothing happened to disturb the peace. Katanga was back in the Central Government's fold, although the northern area was still in the throes of civil rebellion.

Shortly afterwards parts of Kivu suddenly erupted when supporters of the Lumumbast regime came to power in certain districts. The regime was still spreading its tentacles in Kivu. Lagache had heard sporadic reports that Lumumba's National Congolese Movement, in league with the so-called People's Army of Liberation, was active in neighbouring districts. Until recently Lagache had ignored the rumours for lack of true evidence. Now he wondered whether he had done right.

Lagache reduced speed to cross a small wooden bridge at the bottom of a steep rocky escarpment. Then he slapped the Land Rover into low gear and gunned the vehicle up the escarpment and into Kele village. He halted outside a mud-bricked thatched hut, placed in line with similar huts on each side of the crude track the only road from Albertville to Uvira, until Albertville became 'rebel', and the lake level rose six feet, submerging the road completely some thirty kilometres north of Lukamba.

Lagache wiped his forehead with a grubby handkerchief and looked along the two rows of huts. His eyes fell on one of Chief Lufundisha's wives. She was busily pounding manioc roots to a white powder in a primitive wooden bowl with a heavy blunted pole – a process dating back through the centuries to pre-Christian times.

Scarcely aware of the ever-pervading odours that linger in all Congolese villages, Lagache stepped from the Land Rover and walked towards the semi-nude woman. Three of her children were playing near the entrance of Chief Lufundisha's main hut. They gazed up at Lagache, smiling. He stooped and gently patted the nearest child's head, then he turned to the woman and asked in Swahili whether Chief Lufundisha was at home. She shook her head and told him that the chief had gone into the hills with two of the villagers.

In reply, Lagache informed her that he had seen Chief Lufundisha only that morning and he had given no indication of leaving Kele. The woman shrugged her bare shoulders

'The chief returns tomorrow, Bwana,' she said.

Her answer irritated him. 'Where is he in the hills?' he asked, trying to speak calmly.

'I don't know, Bwana.'

She began crushing the manioc roots again. He glared at her, it was on the tip of his tongue to call her a liar, but he stifled the feeling. Instead, he sought solace in a cigarette. He took out a packet of Belga Rouge, extracted a cigarette, lit it and replaced the packet in the breast pocket in his bush shirt. He drew on the cigarette and wondered why the chief should go into the hills at such an inopportune time. He could see other people in the village, mostly women, but at the far end he saw four men. They were squatting on their haunches in a semicircle. Lagache decided to try them.

He strolled towards them pretending that all was well with the world. They were passing a long-stemmed pipe between them. As he came nearer, he could smell the mixture emitted in billowing clouds from the shuttling pipe. It didn't surprise him that they were smoking dagga, the drug plant grew abundantly in the Congo and was just as popular as tobacco among the urban community.

The pipe continued to be passed around as they exchanged greetings with Lagache. He broached them on the subject of Chief Lufundisha's whereabouts. One of them volunteered the information that a runner from Lumbi village arrived in Kele about three hours ago. Apparently, he told Chief Lufundisha that he must go at once to Chief Asana Mussa, the paramount chief of the Mbembe tribe.

Lumbi village, thought Lagache. At least three hours' journey from Kele. Five hours for a white man. No roads led to Lumbi, only a footpath. Lagache didn't favour walking that distance, seeing it, wouldn't serve any purpose if Lufundisha had been summoned to meet his superior.

He returned to his Land Rover and sat behind the wheel, smoking his cigarette, trying to think what he should do next. The woman he had seen first on his arrival in the village had finished crushing the manioc roots. He watched her add water to the fine white powder until it transformed into a grey gluey substance. When the substance hardened, she would cut it into portions for baking. To Europeans the finished product was tasteless to the point of being inedible. To the Congolese, however, it formed a large part of their staple diet.

The three children darted towards the bowl. They dipped their fingers into the grey paste and sampled it. The woman shouted angrily and chased them away. An idea struck Lagache. He would try Father Hubert.

Father Hubert ran the Catholic Mission a few kilometres down the road. There was a possibility that he might know something. In any case Lagache owed him a visit. He flicked away the half-smoked cigarette and started the engine. The three children waved goodbye as he drove from the village.

The Catholic Mission comprised of a chapel, sickbay and a large classroom with Father Hubert's living quarters attached to the sickbay. Every building had a corrugated-tin roof and the walls were built of sun-baked mud bricks. The mission was laid out in an L shape on raised ground and, from the courtyard it was possible to glimpse Lake Tanganyika through the flowering shrubs and slim trunks of the pawpaw trees growing on the lower slopes.

Lagache drove into the courtyard. The priest appeared from behind the chapel with a garden hoe in his hand. As ever, he wore a white cassock over his massive frame. The priest's eyes bulged slightly from a thyroid condition. Lagache noticed that he wasn't his normal cheerful self as he went to meet him.

'Nice to see you, Paul,' he said. 'Let's go into the house. The sun's too hot to stay outside.' The priest saw Lagache glancing at the hoe and smiled. 'My boy failed to come today to hoe the groundnut patch, so I've been doing it myself. But that's the least of my worries.' He pointed the hoe at the classroom. 'Empty, completely empty.'

'It always is in the afternoon, surely,' said Lagache, crossing the threshold of Father Hubert's simple home. 'You give lessons only in the morning, don't you?'

'Quite, but none of my pupils came this morning.' He went to a cabinet and brought out a bottle of brandy and two glasses. He held the bottle up to the light. 'Enough here for two glasses. Last of my stock until the steamer calls at Lukamba again.'

'Don't worry, I'll bring you a bottle tomorrow,' promised Lagache.

Father Hubert poured two equal measures and handed one of the glasses to Lagache. The planter accepted it gratefully. They toasted each other silently and drank. Lagache placed his glass on a table. 'Why didn't you have any pupils this morning, Father?'

'I don't know,' he shrugged. Anyhow that's my problem.'

'Maybe not. It could be mine too.'

The priest sat down in a cane chair and placed his drink on the floor next to him. He looked hard at Lagache.

'This isn't a social call, is it Paul?'

'Not really,' said Lagache, perching himself on the edge of the table. 'There's something strange happening here.'

'Such as?'

'The Kele villagers for example. They're not over enthusiastic in helping my boys gather in the coffee crop. What's more alarming is that my boys are working like a crowd of zombies. You know what this could mean if it continues.'

'A couple of things, I suppose. One – you won't get the best price for your crop. Two – the rebellion is spreading and an African caught helping a European could land in serious trouble.' Father Hubert clamped an empty pipe in his mouth. 'Do you agree?'

'To a certain extent, I do. I'm not sure about the rebellion having spread this far. It could be a case of plain bullying, coupled with political threats. But nothing more than that.'

'Sorry, Paul. You've lost me,' said the priest, filling his pipe bowl with coarse tobacco.

'Not long ago I sacked one of my staff for stealing,' began Lagache. 'This thief was also a troublemaker in more senses than one. You see, Father, I caught him making a pass at Marie a week before I got rid of him.'

'What was your reaction?'

'About Marie?' Father Hubert nodded. 'I clouted him hard. I told him that if he tried anything like that again I would personally throw him off the plantation. When I also found he was a thief I carried out my promise.'

The priest lit his pipe. 'This man must exert a lot of influence if you blame him for everything.'

'Perhaps I'm being stupid about it. On the other hand, he was a nasty piece of work. I really can't understand myself employing him in the first place. On a few occasions I overheard him lecturing my staff on unity, solidarity and fraternity. My guess is that he was a rabid Lumumba supporter,' added Lagache.

'His name?'

'Louis Kimbiti.'

'I think I know him. Doesn't he live at Kele?'

'He was living there when I fired him. I don't know whether he's still living in Kele now. I've never bothered to find out. He lived in Albertville for a couple of years, only returning to Kele at the beginning of this year. That's when he began working for me. After living in Albertville for some time, I suppose he thought he was big enough to try his luck with Marie.'

'The city-type mentality, eh?'

'That's about it,' affirmed Lagache.

Father Hubert knew Marie well. She was a Congolese woman of social standing whom Lagache married four years ago in Bukavu. Lagache was ten years older than Marie, but the age gap was of no consequence. Nor was the difference in ethnicity.

'So, you think that Kimbiti could be the cause of your present troubles?'

'Kimbiti is a lout. He could be threatening my boys. He could also be smearing my character in Kele village so much that the villagers are reluctant, to work for me.'

'Surely you're overestimating this fellow's capabilities. The villagers know you better than to believe a pack of lies from Louis Kimbiti. What's more to the point, Chief Lufundisha would come down on him like a ton of bricks if Kimbiti started slandering you in Kele.'

'If he isn't at the root of the matter, then it must be threats of some nature. Probably political threats.'

'Which brings us back to my original theory.'

'And why nobody attended classes today,' put in Lagache.

'Quite. I waited in that wretched classroom all morning. When it was patently obvious my pupils weren't coming, I went into Kele – lo and behold, there were the kids large as life.'

'What did you do?'

'The obvious. I asked some of the parents why their children were absent from school. The answer I received was that there weren't any lessons today. I then went to Chief Lufundisha's hut for an explanation, but he had left the village thirty minutes earlier.'

'I went to Kele before coming here,' said Lagache. 'Apparently, he's visiting the paramount chief somewhere in the hills, probably at Lumbi. A damned pity – I meant to get Lufundisha into a corner and bribe the truth out of him.'

'All I can suggest is that we wait for him to return. After all, there might just be a simple explanation covering both situations.'

'If there isn't?'

'Let's cross that bridge after we've seen Chief Lufundisha,' replied the priest. 'His trip to the paramount chief might have something to do with this mystery.'

Lagache drank the remaining brandy in his glass and stood up.

'I'm returning to the plantation,' he said. Father Hubert began to rise from his chair, but Lagache waved him back. 'Don't worry, I'll see myself out. Lufundisha should be back in Kele by tomorrow morning. I'm going there about ten o'clock. Perhaps it would be a good idea if you can be in Kele at that time Father.'

Father Hubert removed the pipe from his mouth.

'Very well, Paul. I'll make it my business to be there at ten O'clock. God be with you'

'Thank you.'

The priest heard the roar of Lagache's Land Rover fade in the distance. He rose from his chair, collected Lagache's empty glass and took it to the sink. He failed to hear to door opening slowly behind him.

Marie was waiting for him on the veranda steps when Lagache returned to his home.

'Been to Kele again?' she asked.

He kissed her forehead.

'Yes, but still no luck.'

Rather plump but with a good humoured streak in her character, Marie had appealed to Lagache at their first meeting in a medical clinic at Uvera. Marie was his nurse when he was recuperating from a nasty bout of malaria. Lagache had no prejudices about marrying an African woman. He realised his personal circumstances demanded it. Very few European women relished a lifetime in the bush. Like other Belgians in the same predicament, it was an African woman or nothing. It was, therefore, a simple choice. He married Marie and much to his inner surprise did not regret it.

He placed an arm around her shoulders and they walked inside the bungalow and into the lounge. The lounge stretched the width of the bungalow, its walls festooned with Africana bric-a-brac with colourful rugs casually laid on the polished wooden floor. The furniture was practical and comfortable. The one and only bedroom was at the front of the bungalow. Unlike the lounge, it did not run the full width and was only half the size. The kitchen and bathroom shared the other half, the bathroom being solely accessible from the bedroom.

'Sit down, Paul, I'll get you a beer.' Marie said.

Lagache nodded his appreciation. He sat down on the settee, thinking hard. Marie returned with a foaming tankard of beer, putting it in front of him on a low-slung coffee table. Lagache reached out and gently gripped her wrist, as she withdrew her hand from the tankard.

His action startled her. Her skin felt clammy and Lagache was conscious of her fast pulse rate beating beneath his thumb.

'You're frightened of something, Marie.'

Marie averted her dark eyes as he studied her face.

'Of course, I'm frightened,' she whispered. 'I'm frightened that you will lose your crops.'

Lagache shook his head.

'No, it's more than that, Marie. I can sense it. Tell me what it is, Marie.'

She swallowed hard. 'I wish I knew. I honestly wish I knew, Paul. There's just an air of uncertainty around here, and it scares me. I'm not being stupid – am I?'

She looked at him. Her eyes pleading for confirmation.

'I don't think so,' he answered, releasing her wrist.

Marie moved around the table and sat beside him. They fell silent and the harsh rasping of the crickets outside could be clearly heard above the monotonous chugging of the petrol-driven generator, anchored to the concrete floor in one of the outhouses across the back yard.

The westering sun filtered through the rear window of the lounge, tinting the white walls with a warm pink hue. Within minutes darkness would sweep across the land.

Lagache anticipated it by getting up and switching on the light. Then he drew both sets of curtains across the windows before returning to

Marie's side. The day was still moderately warm and yet he shivered. He frowned angrily as he picked up the tankard. He drank half its contents before setting the tankard down on the table again. *Oh God,* he thought. *What is happening?*

'Give me a cigarette, Paul.'

He passed her his pack of cigarettes. Marie extracted one and he lit it for her. 'Have you found out anything from the boys?' he inquired.

'They'd tell you before they told me, I'm not a Mbembe.'

'I guess you're right.'

The roots of tribalism still ran deep in the area.

'How about Sade?' he suggested, referring to their house boy.

'Sade doesn't say much to me at the best of times.' Marie gave a tired smile. 'Wrong tribe again I suppose.' She picked up a copper ashtray and crushed her cigarette in it. 'I'm sure he knows nothing. He wouldn't keep a secret from you.'

Lagache grunted an affirmative. It was true. Sade had been in the family's employ since the founding of the plantation. The old servant should have been pensioned off some time ago, but when Lagache made the offer Sade refused to hear of such a thing.

'Where's Sade now?'

'Preparing dinner.' They heard the kitchen door latch click up, followed by the dull clang of a saucepan being placed on the large paraffin stove. 'That's him.'

Ordinarily, Lagache would have accepted his wife's word without comment, but he wanted to be sure it was Sade in there. He left Marie on the settee and went to the kitchen door. He opened the door and saw Sade crouched over the stove. As usual he was wearing his impeccably ironed white jacket with gleaming brass buttons.

'Evening Sade,' spoke up Lagache. 'How's the dinner?'

'Nearly ready, Bwana.'

'Glad to hear it. I'm starving.'

He watched Sade tip a mound of peeled potatoes into an iron pot, then he heard Marie moving about in the lounge. She was busily shifting his ledgers from the table in readiness for Sade to lay the cloth and arrange the cutlery. Lagache smiled. Some day he must build that office which he kept on postponing in favour of more urgent work.

His smile faded as he heard the generator splutter to a halt. Then the bungalow lights failed, plunging every room into darkness.

'Dammit,' muttered Lagache, fumbling for his cigarette lighter. He heard Marie say something. 'It's all right.' he called. 'The generator's broken down again. I'm on my way to fix it.'

He struck his lighter and then spoke to Sade. 'Get some candles and take them into the lounge.'

The old servant moved towards the kitchen cupboard. Lagache, meanwhile, slid open a drawer with his free hand and hunted for an adjustable spanner. The lighter began to get unbearably hot in his hand.

'The torch is in the cupboard,' announced Sade.

'Then switch the damn thing on before my hand melts.' A beam of light flashed across the kitchen. 'Ah, that's better,' breathed Lagache, extinguishing his lighter.

He took the torch from Sade, allowing his house boy to light a candle and take it through to the lounge. Then Lagache returned to his search for the spanner. He finally discovered it at the back of the drawer. He grabbed it and then hurried across to the outhouse where the defunct generator was installed.

Lagache didn't bother to switch on the torch as the night sky was comparatively clear. Halfway across the yard he changed his mind. He stopped in his tracks and flashed the torch around, trying to trace a gushing noise. It sounded as though someone had left a tap running. He couldn't detect the source, so he continued on his way. To his astonishment the noise increased as he neared the outhouse. Then he froze, his nostrils twitching.

'Holy Mother! Petrol'

He ran to the outhouse and wrenched the door open. A miniature tide of petrol swept over his boots. He shone the torch on to the generator and saw that a fractured fuel pipe was causing the trouble. The fumes caught his throat, making him cough. He splashed towards the generator and shut off the flow from the fuel tank. The escaping petrol immediately decreased to a mere trickle.

'Now what made that pipe break like that?' he muttered, stepping back. Something hard jabbed against his spine. He gave a surprised grunt.

'Stand still, Monsieur Lagache. Stand very still.'

'Eh?' queried the planter, startled and a little scared.

'Stand still,' repeated the voice.

'Who the hell are you?' he asked angrily, trying to mask his panicky feelings. The thing in his back was removed.

'You can turn round now but make a stupid move and I'll kill you. Understand?'

'I understand all right,' Lagache, replied, gritting his teeth in a mixture of fury and fear.

'Before you turn round, pass your torch to me over your shoulder.' Lagache obeyed. The torch was taken from him and then switched off. He turned to view his antagonist.

A cloud obscured the moon at that precise moment. All Lagache could see was a dark outline of the man. The cloud moved on and his eye caught the metallic glint of a revolver in the man's hand. His heart skipped a couple of beats as the moonlight etched out the man's features.

'You!' he said bitingly. 'What the hell do you want here?'

'So, you haven't forgotten me?'

'How could I?' muttered Lagache.

The man gave a cold, brief laugh. 'Yes, how could you? I've returned, Lagache. Not as your underling, but at the head of the advance force of the People's Army of Liberation. You are now being addressed by Major Louis Kimbiti. For your interest, Lagache, this area is now under my command.'

Lagache stared at Kimbiti through the night as his dazed mind tried to grasp the situation. Major Kimbiti… People's Army of Liberation… the area under the command of this trouble-maker whom he had sacked and was now his prisoner. It was too much of a bad dream to be true.

The moon glowed yellow in the night sky. Lagache noticed the peaked cap which Kimbiti wore. It looked too large for Kimbiti's head and appeared to rest on the ears. The planter guessed that Kimbiti's peaked cap represented his badge of rank. Big hat, big gun, big man. Typical, thought Lagache.

'You'll regret this action in the days to come. Mark my words,' cautioned Lagache.

'I'll what?' said Kimbiti in mock amazement. He raised the revolver until it pointed at Lagache's head. 'Say that again – just say that again!'

'You'll regret this,' said Lagache, his nerves on edge.

The revolver belched flame. Lagache flinched as the bullet screamed past his head.

'Next time it'll aim straight at your mouth, you mangy imperialistic bastard! Now towards the house.'

He hesitated. His body trembling from the shock of being made a target for Kimbiti's gun.

'I said – walk,' roared Kimbiti for the second time.

The full realisation of his predicament hit the planter with the force of a steam-hammer. No longer a mystery, the jigsaw puzzle was shaping all too quickly. Lagache began walking to his bungalow.

He slowed his pace as he neared the back door leading into the kitchen. He thought about chancing Kimbiti's gun and dashing into the kitchen, slamming the door and locking it. The revolver was pushed into his back as Kimbiti ordered him to hurry. Lagache dismissed the escape plan as completely futile. At that range Kimbiti would have no trouble in shooting him down. Lagache stumbled over the threshold and into the kitchen. Sade was nowhere to be seen.

He walked through the kitchen and into the candle-lit lounge with Kimbiti close behind him. He saw Marie crouched up at one end of the settee, looking terrified. She had reason to be; three of Kimbiti's men kept her company. One rebel cradled a Belgian Army Mauser rifle in his arms. The other two rebels, both teenagers, were armed with razor sharp pangas.

Lagache took the perilous situation in at one glance. He noted that the three rebels stared at him in a peculiar way. Their wide staring eyes told him the reason. They were as high on drugs as it was possible to be. Lagache saw the still form of Sade half hidden behind the settee.

'Sit down, pig,' ordered Kimbiti.

He sat down next to his wife and placed a reassuring hand on her thigh. He could have saved himself the effort. Her drawn features, coupled with the violently shivering limb under his hand told him that she was past the reassuring stage. Lagache gestured at the still body of Sade.

'Have you killed him, Kimbiti?' he asked in a soft, but malevolent voice.

Kimbiti kicked the coffee table aside and moved nearer to Lagache and Marie. He leaned forward and shoved his face close to Lagache's. 'I didn't hear you. Tell me again.'

Lagache sensed the taut atmosphere in the room but disregarded it. Now that the posture of events was self-evident, his initial reaction was slowly changing to that of anger.

'I asked you whether you've killed my boy.'

His face jerked sideways as Kimbiti's revolver barrel connected with his left cheekbone. 'My name is Major Kimbiti!' screamed Kimbiti in a fit of rage. 'Have you killed him *Major*? That's what you say, you flea-ridden dog! Have you killed him, *Major*? Understand!'

Lagache rubbed his tender cheek. He would dearly love to smash a fist against Kimbiti's jutting jaw. He checked himself in time and returned Kimbiti's stare. 'Well,' he said at length 'Have you, Major?'

Kimbiti glanced at his three henchmen.

'Well?' he barked. 'Is he dead?'

The rebel holding the Mauser rifle shook his head and patted the butt. 'Unconscious, Major. I knocked him unconscious.'

Kimbiti turned to Lagache. 'Your lapdog's alive. Satisfied?'

'Yes, now why have you come to my plantation. You must.....'

'This plantation is no longer yours,' interrupted Kimbiti, 'It is now my headquarters.'

Again, the planter just managed to control his temper. He realised his only course was to humour Kimbiti until he could gain the upper hand.

'Why this place?'

Kimbiti grinned maliciously. 'For various reasons.'

Lagache's right eyebrow arched quizzically. He would love to know the reasons. Somehow, he judged that he was one of them. A disturbing thought. He scrutinised Kimbiti. 'Surely you must know that you're taking a big risk in coming here.' Kimbiti glared at him. 'Major.' Lagache added, dutifully.

'If you mean I'm risking the Central Government's wrath you can forget it,' came the sneering reply. 'The Central Government is a senile jackal without teeth. Its soldiers do not have a cause. No cause, no fight. Simple as that. They retreat whenever they're confronted with the People's Army of Liberation.'

'I'm just thinking of this district,' interjected Lagache. 'Sooner or later, someone will come here and discover you. It could be a member of my staff, someone from Kele or one of the other villages. Maybe Father Hubert will visit me tomorrow, therefore how can you hold us indefinitely without...' Lagache's voice trailed off when Kimbiti and his men sniggered in unison.

'Your dog-like head has as much brain as a rotting melon,' announced Kimbiti. He spoke slowly to allow the insults to sink home. 'You didn't hear me properly when I first told you outside. Seeing that you belong to such a corrupt nation, I suppose I must make allowances and tell you again.' He paused momentarily for effect, then continued. 'This area is under the jurisdiction of the People's Army of Liberation. By area, I mean forty kilometres to the north and forty to the south of here. Moreover, I'm the revolutionary officer commanding this area, including the town of Lukamba.'

'And what about the Provincial Government?'

'What Provincial Government?' said Kimbiti, scornfully. 'As far as we're concerned, the People's Army is the Provincial Government.'

'I bet Chief Lufundisha will have something to say when he hears that,' returned Lagache, steadily. He felt Marie's hand slide beneath his own. He squeezed her hand gently to give her hope. He observed Kimbiti grinning again.

'Chief Lufundisha isn't in any position to comment,' smirked Kimbiti. 'He was killed in the hills a few hours ago.'

'In other words, he walked into a trap.'

'You could say that, but why worry about Lufundisha? You should be worrying about yourselves.' He leered at Marie. Lagache felt her muscles go tense. She stifled a sob. The planter coldly ignored the insinuation. Kimbiti changed the subject. 'Where do you keep your drink?' He glanced around the lounge but failed to see the cocktail cabinet at the rear of him. 'Come on Lagache. Revolutions make men thirsty.'

'You surprise me,' retorted Lagache, making the most of Kimbiti's lack of surveillance to look around himself for some sort of an escape route. Kimbiti's power-mad eyes swung back to Lagache.

'I surprise you, do I? Come on – out with it! Where are your drinks? And don't tell us that you haven't any like that priest did.' Lagache's eyes narrowed on hearing Kimbiti mention a priest. 'Unlike him, you're a planter and I've yet to hear of a planter who doesn't drink.'

'Who else?' Kimbiti took notice of Lagache's concerned attitude. He laughed sharply. 'He's dead, dead, dead. There's no room for men like him among us. It's people like him who place thoughts into the minds of my people – thoughts that are opposite to our revolutionary ideals. Letting him live would confuse my people. So, I arranged for him to meet his so-called God.' Kimbiti studied Lagache. 'Why look so sick? You must remember that he's been preparing himself for death, like he has been preparing other idiots. I only made it possible for him to get there faster.'

'You bastard,' hissed Lagache, aghast. 'You jumped-up uncivilised bastard!'

He launched himself at Kimbiti before the self-styled major or his accomplices were aware of his intentions. In blind anger he knocked Kimbiti's revolver to one side and lashed out with his fist. It connected flush with Kimbiti's chin and Lagache had the satisfaction of glimpsing Kimbiti reeling back on to the cocktail cabinet. He heard the discordant notes of glass shattering just as the rebel with the Mauser hit him on the side of the head. He fell across the coffee table which collapsed beneath his weight.

His mind swimming from the rifle blow, he looked up on hearing Marie cry out in horror. He saw a panga in the act of being swung downward in a lethal motion towards his face.

'Don't kill him! Don't kill him!' croaked Kimbiti, staggering to his feet and clasping his jaw Kimbiti waved the now crestfallen rebel away from Lagache and walked with an unsteady gait towards the planter. Lagache tensed his body as Kimbiti's foot went back. The ensuing kick made Lagache grunt in pain. The rebel major kicked him again, in the ribs, for good measure. 'Stay on the ground, Lagache,' ordered Kimbiti, still nursing his jaw. 'Don't imagine you're going to die from a simple panga slash. Death is too final for your breed.'

Marie stood up from the settee, but the teenage rebel who wielded the panga pushed her down again. Her face was a mask of terror. Lagache stayed on the floor with the Mauser rifle trained on him.

Two bottles of imported Scotch whisky had rolled on to the floor after Kimbiti's collision with the cocktail cabinet. Kimbiti picked up both bottles, studied the labels, then tossed one of the bottles to the panga-wielding rebel nearest to Lagache's wife. 'Share that bottle between you,' instructed Kimbiti, commencing to uncork the other bottle.

Lagache watched in icy silence as the bottle went from rebel to rebel, its contents diminishing fast.

Kimbiti drank very conservatively from his bottle and returned it almost full to the top of the cocktail cabinet for further use. Lagache was disappointed that his former plantation boy did not plan to get drunk or even a little tipsy. Escape would be much easier if all four of them became incapacitated through too much drink. Alas, it was not to be. Kimbiti came over to the settee, a thin smile playing on his lips. Lagache's beating heart increased in pitch. One look at Kimbiti told him that the man had stopped playing the cat and mouse game. He grabbed Marie's arm and pulled her away from the settee just before the planter realised Kimbiti's intentions.

'Let her go,' demanded Lagache, beginning to rise to his feet.

'Get hold of him,' said Kimbiti. The rifle butt connected with the back of Lagache's neck, and he sprawled on the floor again.

The two young rebels leapt on him and pinned him to the floor. Kimbiti twisted Marie's right arm behind her back. 'You love your wife, don't you?' said Kimbiti, rhetorically. 'I'm about to show her what happens when a Congolese woman marries a Belgian capitalist.' He pulled Marie's head back and she saw Kimbiti grinning. 'You're coming with me,' he said.

'Where to?' she gasped.

'Not far.' He propelled her towards the bedroom.

'Leave her alone, Kimbiti!' shouted Lagache, helplessly.

He ignored the planter's plea and addressed his men instead. 'You remember what we discussed, start doing it in five minutes time.' With that he dragged Lagache's struggling wife into the bedroom. The door slammed shut behind them.

Shortly afterwards weak cries of help drifted through the closed bedroom door. Wild-eyed, his mind tormented, Lagache strove desperately to free himself from the clutches of his captors. Although drugged and fairly drunk, the three rebels managed to hold him down. One rebel held each of his arms, while the rebel with the rifle pinned his legs. Lagache saw the rebel who held his legs reach forward, grasp the top of his bush shirt and rip it apart, exposing Lagache's chest. Kimbiti's accomplices began to laugh and chuckle as the same rebel produced a small, bladed knife from his belt.

The rebel holding Lagache's left arm tore the planter's watch from his wrist and looked at the dial. 'Another two minutes and we'll begin,' he said.

'Let's start now,' suggested the rebel who had lain his rifle aside for the knife. 'The Major will be busy for some time yet.' He grinned and flourished the knife over Lagache's bare stomach.

A shrill cry came from the bedroom, followed quickly by a sharp slapping sound. Beads of sweat formed on Lagache's brow as he renewed his efforts to struggle free. The blade of the knife broke the skin below his right collarbone and, sick with fear and pain, Lagache felt the rebel describe the shape of a 'S' on his body with the knife. Blood appeared and filled the incision before overflowing and trickling down his right side in tiny rivulets.

The rebel was in the act of cutting the skin again when the bedroom door opened and Kimbiti appeared, buttoning his blue trousers. The rebels glanced around, allowing Lagache to lift his head as far as he was able, trying to see what had been happening in the bedroom. He just managed to distinguish his wife lying on the bed, bare from the waist downwards, before the young rebel holding his left arm pushed his head back against the floor.

'Here,' Kimbiti said to the rebel with the knife. 'Your turn with her.' He sneered and glanced briefly at Lagache. 'She fought like ten leopards, but a few hard slaps put a stop to that.'

Kimbiti took the knife and sat on the planter's legs. He was about to make a remark to Lagache when he noticed Sade groping to his feet. The rebel with whom he had changed places was on the verge of entering the bedroom. 'Get him!' yelled Kimbiti.

The rebel looked round and immediately reached for his rifle. Lagache's servant never really saw the man bound over to him. The rifle butt swung down and smashed against his head with sickening thud. Sade emitted a low moan and collapsed on the floor. His old body shuddered visibly, his hands pawing the rug beneath him, then he died.

His murderer picked up a cushion from the settee and wiped the rifle butt clean. He threw the bloodstained cushion on to Sade's lifeless body and commenced his interrupted walk to the bedroom. Kimbiti began carving an 'I' on Lagache's heaving chest.

By the time the fourth rebel had made the sortie into the bedroom, the planter's chest was a mess of bloodily carved letters. Kimbiti sat back to admire the word SIMBA, and the initials L.K. carved below it. Mercifully, Lagache had fainted halfway through the torture.

'Magnificent,' beamed Kimbiti, standing up. 'Now get some water and throw it over him. I want him to be fully conscious for the final ceremony.'

A bucket of water was brought, in from the kitchen. Kimbiti took it by the handle and poured the whole lot over Lagache's ashen features.

For a few seconds he lay still before spluttering his way to consciousness. As his fogged mind cleared, he became acutely aware of the throbbing pain from his lacerated chest. He struggled into a sitting position and propped himself against the settee. He gazed up at them with dull eyes.

'For God's sake, get me something to bandage my chest,' he implored.

Kimbiti laughed. 'Use your shirt,' he said, callously. He waved a hand towards the bedroom. 'Bring her out here.'

They brought Marie out. She hobbled between them; her naked body almost doubled up as she tried to lessen the burning ache. They halted her a few paces away from Lagache. She raised her head in a jerking movement and looked at him poignantly.

'I tried to stop them. I tried.'

'I know you did, Marie,' he said weakly.

Lagache stumbled to his feet, his own pain forgotten as he tried to reach his ravaged wife. The rebels holding her, pulled her back from him. Then one of the rebels left Marie and grabbed him. Kimbiti spoke: 'Remember your wife, Lagache. Remember her as she looks now. Tell them in Uvira what we have done to you both. Tell them that the People's Army of Liberation, or the Simbas – whatever you wish, will do the same to them if they stay loyal to Leopoldville.'

Lagache's numbed mind failed to grasp the significance of Kimbiti's speech. Uvira? Surely Kimbiti planned to kill him now.

He watched listlessly as Kimbiti's right hand wrapped itself around the revolver butt protruding from his belt.

Yes. He was to be shot. They had no intention of releasing him. Marie, being Congolese and a woman, would probably stay with them to serve as a chattel. He saw Kimbiti raise the revolver with a casualness that belied the dramatic situation. Marie hadn't noticed the new turn of events. She was swaying on her feet, staring at the floor. He closed his eyes, drew a deep breath and waited for death to supersede the nightmare.

There came a deafening report. His mind recoiled instantly. He raised his hands in a feeble gesture to ward off the bullet.

But no bullet came.

It took a little time for the fact to sink in. He opened his eyes. To his utter amazement, he was indeed alive. He smiled stupidly and flashed a look at his wife. Marie was still staring at the floor. Lagache frowned and the stupid smile evaporated from his face. There was something wrong, but he couldn't figure out what.

Kimbiti nodded. The two rebels holding Marie released their grip on her arms. She immediately plunged to the floor. Lagache gazed in horror at the gaping hole in her head, then at the blood and brains on the floor. He fainted for the second time.

Kimbiti shoved the revolver back in his belt.

'Get some more water and revive him. Rip up a sheet and bandage his chest too,' he ordered. 'I don't want him bleeding to death before he gets to Uvira.'

Lagache was vaguely aware of being drenched in water. Then he felt something being wrapped around his chest.

'That's enough,' he heard Kimbiti say. 'Now get him to the Land Rover.'

He felt himself being dragged across the lounge floor and on to the porch. The night air revived him a little. He was bundled with scant ceremony into the back of the Land Rover. The rebels climbed in after him. With Kimbiti at the wheel, they drove down the track behind the bungalow which led to the lake.

Kimbiti pulled up outside Lagache's small boathouse. It then dawned on him how he was to travel to Uvira. He was taken inside and thrown on some sacks. Kimbiti, meanwhile, checked the dinghy which the planter used for fishing purposes. Satisfied, the rebel major pushed Lagache into the boat. Kimbiti turned to the outboard motor and yanked at the cord. The engine growled into life.

Lagache was dimly aware of being ordered to grasp the tiller. Kimbiti stepped out of the dinghy and untied the mooring rope. He drew his revolver and fired a shot into the air. He fired another shot into the water by the dinghy.

'Tell them at Uvira, Lagache. Tell them!' he shouted.

Lagache opened the throttle. Waves slapped against the boathouse in the wake of the craft as Lagache headed towards the middle of the lake. Five hundred metres from the shore he turned to port and set course for Uvira.

As he ploughed through the placid waters, he thought of everything he had lost. Above all he thought of his dead wife, Marie. Someday, he vowed, someone must pay for that atrocity. Moreover, it must be paid in full. In the Congo's realm of new currency. In blood.

CHAPTER THREE

Johannesburg is the fastest growing city in Africa with the fastest wife-swapping district to match its phenomenal growth. It houses one of the most densely populated European areas known – an area located on a brow with the hub of the city squatting below it. Surrounding the hub are the mountainous goldmine dumps, an ever-present reminder of how Johannesburg came into being.

Johannesburg is renowned for its natural wealth of gold. It is also renowned for an unnatural suicide rate and three murders a day.

It is a city of filth, violence and traffic lights. The filth is there to see, the violence lurks in the alleys, and the traffic lights stab the straight streets to death at every corner block.

Johannesburg by day is a whirlpool of people dashing endlessly after bloated pay cheques. At night it dies of exhaustion with only the odd African watchman, huddled over a glowing coal brazier, keeping a sleepy vigil over the silent city.

With Johannesburg, it is a love-hate relationship.

Love it for its material existence. Hate it for its cultural desert. Rarely is there a happy medium.

Roy Morgan hated it. Period.

He preferred the warmth of the Cape and the sauntering atmosphere so prevalent in Cape Town. Every time he became bored with the rat-race environment of Johannesburg, he thought seriously of returning there. The last time he thought about it coincided with a recruitment drive for able-bodied men to serve as mercenaries in the Congo. He immediately dismissed Cape Town from his mind and signed up.

Now he was back after receiving the news of his parents' fatal car crash on the Johannesburg/Pretoria highway.

He arrived too late for their funeral, but in time to pay for it. The monthly rent was too prohibitive for him to stay on at his parents' flat, so ne moved into a bachelor flat in the Johannesburg suburb of Hillbrow.

Morgan found employment three weeks after his move. The work being of a clerical nature wasn't really hard, simply monotonous with little or no chance of promotion.

His short spell in the Congo with its flies, mosquitoes and smells, not to mention rebel bullets, became less of an unpleasant memory as the weeks wore on. And the more he thought of the money he had earned in the Congo, the more he thought about rejoining 5 Commando. One morning at work, when the telephone just wouldn't cease ringing, he made up his mind to take that short walk to Pritchard Street where the recruiting office was housed.

There were four order clerks in the firm, including himself. They worked a lunch hour shift for the benefit of the company's customers. Morgan's lunch hour was from 12:00 until 13:00 hours. Precisely at noon he shoved his chair back and stood up. Tim Bream, the other clerk whose lunch hour also began at noon, did the same.

'Are you going to the pub to eat?' he asked Morgan.

'No, not today. I've got to see to a few things.'

'Surely you've time for a quick beer and sandwich?'

Morgan shook his head. 'I wish I did.'

'Come on, Roy,' persisted Bream, 'I'll pay.'

'Tomorrow, Tim. Tomorrow.'

He walked from the office with Bream trailing behind him. Bream offered him a cigarette as they waited for the lift to arrive. Morgan refused politely.

'No beer, no sandwich and now you don't want, a cigarette.' Bream smiled. 'What is it? Girl trouble?'

'No, nothing like that.'

'I thought not,' said Bream.

Morgan gave him an enquiring look. 'What the hell does that mean?'

The corners of Bream's mouth lifted into a grin. He edged closer to Morgan. 'Tell me, Roy, what were you doing before coming here?'

'Same as here,' he answered cautiously. 'Clerking.'

'That's not what I've heard,' said Bream quietly. He glanced sharply at Bream just as the lift came. The doors slid apart, and they stepped into the lift, the only passengers. Morgan pressed the lower button on the control panel. The doors closed and they began descending to the ground floor. 'I heard you were doing something else.'

'Oh, did you now.'

'Yes, I did,' said Bream equably. He looked at, Morgan. 'Care to tell me about it.'

'Tell you about what?' demanded Morgan in biting tones.

'The Congo,' Bream replied softly.

Morgan froze for a second.

'Now where did you hear that crap?'

'This town's lousy with ex-mercenaries I heard it from two different sources. What's more I believe it. You've never been really keen about your job, have you?'

'That doesn't mean a damn thing,' rasped Morgan. 'There must be thousands of people who aren't interested in their work.'

The lift reached the ground floor, and the doors slid back. They stepped out and walked across the hall to the street entrance.

'I bet you didn't say where you had been when you applied for this job,' rejoined Bream outside the building. Morgan said nothing. 'You needn't worry. I won't tell anyone.' Again, Morgan refused to comment.

Together, they walked along the pavement. Morgan intended crossing the street at the end of the block, leaving Bream to turn right in the direction of his favourite bar. To his consternation, Bream stayed with him. The traffic lights changed, barring his path to the other side of the street.

'I thought you were going to your pub?'

'I am, but I'd like you to tell me about the Congo.'

Morgan swung round angrily. 'Why the hell should I?'

Morgan's outburst put Bream on the defensive. 'I guess you don't have to tell me,' he mumbled hurriedly. 'I'd just, like to know, that's all.'

'Why? Didn't your two sources tell you?' said Morgan, his voice tinged with sarcasm.

'Not really. The Congo didn't interest me then,' he admitted. Morgan stared at him. Bream stared straight back.

'Okay, out with it, Tim. Why does it interest you now?'

'I'm just wondering if it's a feasible proposition,' he said hesitantly.

Morgan's stern features softened. 'You're not thinking of going north, are you?'

It was Bream's turn to feel uncomfortable. Morgan sensed that Bream was making up his mind whether he could trust him. Morgan let him sweat it out.

'Confidentially – yes,' he said at length.

'Aren't you married? What does your wife think about it?'

'She isn't in a position to think about it or to care. You see, we're separated.'

'Oh, I see.' Morgan did not press the point, but added, 'You realise that guys get killed up there?'

'I'll take my chance. Besides, I'm not dim. There's a war on up there and deaths usually go hand in hand with war.'

'Too bloody right they do. Anyhow, what about, your job here?'

'For Christ's sake, Roy, what *about* my job? Sitting at a desk all day, answering a bloody phone and scribbling out orders by the dozen. Hell, man, a well-trained chimp could do that job.'

He unwittingly glared at Morgan. 'I need money, Roy. Big money. My wife cleaned me out of nearly every cent I possess. It would take me ages in this job to save that, amount of money again.'

'How did she manage that?'

'Simple. She took off with my bank balance. She reckoned she had to meet our HP payments and asked me to sign a blank cheque. I was in a hurry, so I signed it without giving it great thought. The bitch drew out all my savings and went away in her boyfriend's car – so I gathered from her note left for me on the kitchen table.'

'Gee, I to sorry to hear that, Tim,' commiserated Morgan with feeling. 'So now you want, to try your luck with 5 Commando? You're really serious about it?'

'Absolutely,' affirmed Bream.

Morgan grinned openly. 'So am I. Strictly between the two of us, I'm on my way to the recruiting office now.'

'No kidding!'

'I want to see if I can sign on for a second contract. It's okay by me if you want to come along too.' He gave Bream a penetrating look. 'That is, of course, if you're still serious. It can get awful rough up there. Well, Tim?'

Bream swallowed hard. His mouth suddenly felt very dry.

'Try stopping me,' he said.

CHAPTER FOUR

Since its inception, the 5 Commando recruiting office had been housed in various Johannesburg business buildings. On the occasion Morgan and Bream visited the place, it was located on the second floor of Pritchard House in Pritchard Street. The two young men walked to the second floor in preference to waiting for the ancient lift to arrive.

The door of the recruiting office was ajar when they reached the second-floor landing. Through the small gap in the door the sound of incoherent conversation drifted to their ears. Morgan glanced swiftly at Bream before rapping his knuckles against the top panel of the badly painted door. The door creaked back enough to allow him a view of two men leaning over a paper-strewn desk at the far end of the office, deep in conversation.

They didn't seem to hear Morgan's knocking. Bream looked over Morgan's shoulder and saw that the office also had a tiny waiting room of sorts, partitioned off immediately on the right-hand side of the main office. Morgan knocked again. This time a small-built man, standing behind the desk, looked up. Even though the desk was twenty feet from the door, Bream couldn't help but notice the man's cold, clear blue eyes. Suddenly he felt apprehensive about the whole business. He wanted a quick word with Morgan, but he was too late. Morgan was already halfway towards the desk. Bream followed like a hypnotic rabbit.

Morgan shook hands briefly with the taller of the two men, before saying a very respectful 'Good afternoon,' to the man with the clear blue eyes.

'Haven't I seen you somewhere before?' asked the man, scrutinising him.

'The name's Morgan, sir. I'm here to see if I can sign on for a second contract.'

Bream saw the small man glance at his companion.

'Morgan hasn't blotted his copybook as far as I know,' came the reply, correctly deciphering the silent enquiry. The small man rubbed his clean-shaven chin. He looked again at Morgan. 'I remember now. Your parents died in a car accident while you were in the Congo. Go into the waiting room. I'll see you in a minute.'

'My friend would like to sign on too, sir.'

Bream felt himself come under the penetrating gaze of the small man.

'Take him with you. I'll interview him after I've seen you, Morgan.'

The waiting room looked positively crowded, although Bream counted only six people. He was surprised to see a young woman among the six occupants. Her face, once beautiful, was prematurely lined and her raven hair hung straight, and cut very severely. Her dress, handbag and shoes seemed cheap enough to have been bought at any chain store. Moreover, they matched each other in colour – black. The only thing bright about her was a wide gold wedding ring. She gave Bream a sideways look when he sat down next to Morgan on a makeshift bench. The woman reminded him of a young witch – a daughter of death. Bream shivered slightly and tried to ignore her presence.

'Who is the small guy out there?' he asked Morgan.

'Commandant Simon Morley. He's 5 Commando's second-in-command. I served under him for a time when he was a machine-g.'

'Looks a bit of a killer to me,' reflected Bream.

'He is, and nothing scares him. He's been wounded Christ knows how many times. Always comes back for more, though.'

'Must be a nutcase,' said Bream in a whisper.

He sneaked a glance along the bench.

Two men sat beside the witch, one of them looked about Morgan's age and the other man – supremely confident of himself – could pass for thirty-four. Bream found it difficult to judge his true age. The bench opposite held two blue-chinned Italians, also a scruffily dressed man of indeterminate nationality.

'Roy,' whispered Bream, nudging his friend, 'What's the name of the bloke with Morley?'

'Fry, I think.'

'Someone want me?' came a voice.

'No, it's okay,' said Morgan quickly, as Fry entered the waiting room holding a batch of printed cards.

'Good, now fill these in and return them to me when your turn comes,' said Fry, handing three to Morgan. He turned to Bream and gave him three cards as well. Bream saw that they were identical application forms. The mercenary officer gazed around the room. 'Where is Mr Ashton?'

'Here,' murmured the man whom Bream had had trouble in deducing the correct age.

'Completed your forms, Mr Ashton? You have? Ah, thank you. Now would you please step this way.'

Toby Ashton stood up and flicked an imaginary speck of dust from his bespoke Richard Audsley suit as he went into the main office.

His application cards were placed in front of Commandant Morley, and he was asked to sit in the chair facing the mercenary officer.

'Now, Mr Ashton,' began Morley in a dour accent as he ran his eyes down the completed application forms, 'I see that you're English and have served in the Royal Navy.'

'Yes,' said Ashton, slightly amused how a fellow with Morley's accent could get so far. Obviously conducted himself well in the field, he thought. He looked at Morley. 'Does it, matter much whether a chap's only had naval service as against army experience?'

Morley shook his head. 'We also have a navy, Mr Ashton,' he grinned at Fry who was standing next to the desk. 'Probably bigger than the South African Navy. Eh, Machine-g?'

Fry laughed. 'It could well be.'

The grin vanished from Morley's face quicker than it had appeared. He scrutinised the application forms again. 'You were a lieutenant.'

'I was indeed.'

'Have you got your discharge papers to verify your rank?'

Toby Ashton coughed politely behind his right hand.

'I'm afraid not,' he replied apologetically, 'I lost many of my personal papers in a fire just after the war, including my ex-naval documents. My commission was gazetted in April 1946 if that will help you.'

He failed to mention that the findings of his Court Martial were gazetted in late 1949. He was thankful that the commandant appeared satisfied with his answer.

'We can use you in our navy on Lake Tanganyika. Are you interested?'

'I am,' Ashton assured him.

'Good. There's a chartered aircraft leaving Jan Smuts Airport at midnight, this coming Sunday. See that you have smallpox and yellow fever vaccination certificates. Make sure your passport is in order too. Don't take a heavy suitcase. All you really need is your toilet kit, plenty of razor blades, change of underclothes and a pair of bathing trunks if you wish. Report here on Friday with your passport and vaccination certificates for a final briefing.' Morley gave Ashton's expensive suit a cursory glance. 'I'd advise you to travel in casual clothing too. The climate up there rots fabric like nobody's business. Any questions?'

'Just one,' said Ashton hopefully. 'The salary?'

'£140 a month basic with £150 on top when you're in the danger area. £7,000 goes to your nearest kin should you have the misfortune in getting yourself killed. Satisfied?'

'I should say so.'

'We must have a medical certificate to show that you are a fit man. Bring it along with you on Friday.' Morley glanced at Fry. 'Let me have the next applicant.'

Ashton left the recruiting office and stepped jauntily down the stairs, feeling very pleased with himself.

Bream completed his application forms and sat back looking contented. They certainly wanted to know a lot of information he thought, lighting a cigarette. How old he was, where he lived, whether single, married or divorced. Who and where his parents were born, their names and nationality. His military experience, particular blood group and religion. He had answered everything to the best of his ability. Now it was just a question of waiting to see this Commandant Morley.

Morgan had also completed his forms. He returned his pen to his top pocket and gratefully accepted a cigarette from his friend. He lit up just as another man walked in to take the seat vacated by Ashton. They immediately recognised each other.

'Jannie Gerber!' exclaimed Morgan, jumping up. 'Don't tell me you want to sign on again?'

'Sure, I do, Roy. If Morley lets me,' said Gerber, lifting his left hand.

Bream's eyes widened in horror on seeing Gerber's hand. Only the thumb and little finger remained. The other three fingers had been amputated totally and utterly, leaving a ghastly layer of deep pink flesh in their place.

'What do you think your chances are with Morley?' asked Morgan in sympathetic tones.

'Personally speaking, I don't see why he should stop me. This wound is more or less healed now. Besides, can still fire an F.N.' Gerber added, holding up his undamaged right hand.

'What about your compensation, Jannie. Has it come through yet?'

'Not yet,' he admitted.

'Then why go up again?' snapped the woman in black.

Her bleak question surprised everybody in the room.

Gerber shrugged his shoulders. 'Because I want to, I guess,' he said lamely.

Fry poked his head into the waiting room. 'Filled in your forms, Morgan?'

'Yes,' said Morgan.

'Okay. Go and see Commandant Morley.'

He went through and Morley waved him into the chair in front of the desk.

'All right, let me have 'em,' said Morley, briskly tapping the desk. Morgan handed over his application forms and the mercenary officer quickly studied them.

'It looks as though you've answered everything,' he announced, tossing the forms across to Fry. 'There's a plane leaving for Albertville on Sunday. Can you make it?'

'I can, sir,' said Morgan with conviction.

'You'll find that the scene's changed somewhat. This particular contract is for the Baraka area on Lake Tanganyika. The cowboy days finished on Baraka's capture. You'll find yourself foot-slogging more often than riding. A lot has changed in twelve months, make no mistake.'

'Well, I guess that's progress,' put in Morgan, 'but I'm still willing.'

'Good, now call in here on Friday for a final briefing. Don't forget to bring your passport, smallpox and yellow fever vaccination certificates plus a medical certificate from your doctor,' Morley broke off and swore softly. He looked at Fry.

'We forgot to tell that character Ashton about photographs. What address has he given us?'

Fry shuffled through the application forms until he found Ashton's. 'Hmm,' mused Fry with a smile. 'He's staying at the Langham.'

'Fancies himself, doesn't he,' grunted Morley. 'Phone the hotel, Machine-g, and try to contact him. If he isn't in, then leave a message for him to contact us.'

Morley shoved the telephone towards Fry and then turned his attention to Morgan again.

'We need three passport-size photographs from you for your application forms. Understand?'

'Yes, sir.'

'Bring them in with you on Friday with the other bumf. Now ask your friend to come here.'

A little shaken by his abrupt dismissal from Morley's desk, Morgan returned to the waiting room. 'The Commandant wants to see you,' he said to Bream, unaware of the glowering looks coming from the two Italians for jumping the queue. The woman, however, continued sitting like a rock and was equally mute. Bream went in the main office, feverishly clutching his application forms. Morley made him sit down and asked him for his forms. Morley took them with an indifferent attitude and commenced checking the details.

'So, you're twenty-three, South African and married,' observed Morley.

'Actually I'm separated,' explained Bream.

'But not divorced?'

'No. At least not yet,' he added hurriedly.

'If you let us have your marriage certificate, we'll arrange for you to claim marriage allowance. That's an extra £20 a month.'

'Hell, that's worth having,' said Bream. He was about to thank Morley when the mercenary officer's cold fishy eyes seemed to pin him to the chair.

'But you can't get the allowance until we have your marriage certificate. Understand.'

'Yes, yes, of course.'

Morley looked down at the application forms again. 'Nine months service in the Citizens' Defence Force. Did you manage to get promotion?'

'No, I didn't attain any rank.'

'At least you're honest,' rumbled Morley. 'If you can make Sunday's flight, you can join. Your friend Morgan will tell you what we require in the way of documents. Make sure you have them with you when you come here on Friday.'

'On Friday?'

'Morgan knows about it. Now when you go back to the waiting room, ask that woman to come out here.'

'What are you going to say to her?' said Fry to Morley as Bream returned to the waiting room.

'That her husband died a man's death.' A smile flickered on Morley's pale lips, 'I can hardly tell her that he drowned himself in a trench latrine after a night on palm beer, now, can I?'

Fry gave a short laugh. The woman in black emerged from the waiting room. His laugh turned to a cough as he pretended to clear his throat. The woman walked towards Morley. The mercenary officer asked her to sit down.

'I suppose you want to know how your husband died, Mrs Viljoen,' began Morley sombrely.

'Not really,' she snapped. 'He couldn't give a damn about me when he was alive, and I'm not going to lose much sleep now that he's dead.'

Morley arched his eyebrows in surprise. 'Then why are you here?'

'For the compensation money. What else?'

'What else, indeed?' Morley murmured below his breath. He glanced at Fry and then at her.

'I'll notify you when your money comes through,' he said.

'Make it soon. I want a holiday. Goodbye, Mr Morley.'

Fry gaped in disbelief as she stalked out of the door. 'Christ!' he said, recovering his composure.

Morley chuckled softly. 'I wish they were all like that. Our lives would be far less complicated. Remind me to phone her as soon as we hear. I'd hate to hold up her holiday plans.'

'Don't worry. I will. Let's hope it comes through before you go north. I don't want to be alone in this office when she comes again. She scares the hell out of me.'

'Probably scared the hell out of her husband too,' said Morley, lighting a cigarette. 'Okay, send the next one in.'

Bream scribbled down the documents he had to obtain when he and Morgan were in the street outside the recruiting office. He then looked at his watch and gasped.

'Roy it's way past our lunch hour.'

'So what? I'm not going back today or any other day.'

Bream stared at him in astonishment. 'Not even to tell 'em that you're leaving?'

'Nope,' replied Morgan with alacrity. 'They can find out in their own sweet time.'

'Well, I don't know,' said Bream dubiously.

Morgan cut him short. 'Forget about me. Think about yourself. You've got to see your doctor for a check-up, get the necessary jabs and have your ugly face photographed – all by Friday morning. I suggest you begin now, otherwise you might not make it.'

Bream smiled nervously. 'Okay, you've talked me into it. I'll see you later, maybe.'

Morgan grinned. 'Maybe.'

He watched Bream turn the corner, then he stepped back and bumped into somebody.

'Can't you look where you're going?' said a female voice.

He turned round and came face to face with the woman in black. She looked at him curiously. 'Weren't you upstairs just now?'

'Yes, I was.'

'Are you really signing on for the Congo? My husband was killed up there you know.'

'I'm sorry to hear that.'

'Oh, don't be.'

'Any children?' he asked as he began walking up the street with her. He noticed her face soften.

'None. I didn't think he would stick around, so I took precautions.' She glanced at him as they walked along. 'It's the truth, so I might as well admit it.'

'I suppose you're living with your parents now.'

'They're down in the Cape. I live in a flat by myself a couple of blocks from here.'

'I'll walk with you. I'm going that way.'

She looked at him sharply. She was about to say something but changed her mind. 'If you want to.'

Morgan ran a finger around the inside of his collar. 'Gee I wish the bars were open. That recruiting office was like an oven.'

'Save your money,' she retorted. 'You can have a drink at my place. The only thing my husband left me was bottles. Most of them empty, but you can have a full one with my compliments.'

She stopped outside a block of flats that was old by Johannesburg standards. He followed her into a cramped lift which creaked its way up to the fourth floor. Morgan pulled back the gates to let her out. There were eight identically painted doors leading to flats along the passage from the lift.

'Which is your flat?' he asked.

'This one,' she said, standing in front of the third door and fumbling in her handbag for the key. She unlocked the door and Morgan peered over her shoulder into the flat as she pushed the door open. It was a one-room affair with the bathroom and kitchen opposite each other in the small corridor which led to a large room in the rear. 'It's not a palace, but it'll do until the compensation money comes through,' she added, closing the front door behind Morgan.

He walked through to the large room which served as the lounge and bedroom. The room was sparsely furnished, just a table, two dining chairs, two easy chairs and a divan bed hard against one of the walls. Nearby the bed was a heavily varnished chest of drawers with a large mirror on top. In front of the mirror stood a bowl of flowers. The carpet beneath Morgan's feet was clean, but distinctly threadbare.

'Switch on the radio. This place depresses me when it's so silent,' she said, pointing to a portable radio on the table. 'I'm going to see what's in the kitchen.'

Morgan picked up the radio and tuned in to a music programme. He replaced the radio on the table and wandered into the kitchen. He saw her bending over a collection of bottles in the far corner.

The hem of her skirt had ridden halfway up her thighs, showing a pair of nicely shaped legs. He was still admiring them as she straightened up, holding a bottle of Castle lager.

'Will this do?' she enquired.

'Just fine,' he replied, taking the bottle.

'I feel thirsty too, so leave me some. You'll find glasses in the cupboard and an opener in the kitchen drawer. I'll join you in a minute.'

He took down two glasses from off the cupboard shelf as she disappeared into the bathroom. He filled both glasses and had taken them into the lounge by the time she reappeared. He offered her one.

'What shall we drink to?' he said.

'For what we are about to receive. What you will earn and what I earned by proxy,' she replied, forcing a laugh.

'A good enough toast.' They clinked glasses and Morgan drained his glass without respite. 'I didn't realise I was so dry,' he declared, seating himself down.

The woman only sipped at her lager. 'It sure makes a change seeing a man around here,' she said, reclining in the other chair. She ran a hand through her hair. 'I guess I'll learn to live without one without turning butch.'

'You don't look lesbian material. Incidentally, my name's Roy. Yours?'

'Rita, but I dare say you'll have forgotten it by Sunday.'

He chuckled. 'You really look on the dark side of things, don't you?'

'Don't blame me for that. My faith in human nature has taken quite a tumble since my marriage. At the time I thought I was doing myself a favour too.'

'What do you mean?'

'My father fancied me more than my mother. Then dream boy came into my life. I married him without giving it much thought. He turned into a nightmare.' She paused and toyed with her glass. 'Still, this money should give me a new start in life.'

'I hope it does.' Morgan stood up to go. 'I've only got a few days left in town. How about you and I going somewhere tonight'

'That sounds nice.'

'Let's say seven this evening – but do me a favour?'

'If I can.'

'Get out of those widow's weeds and wear something attractive. Black is not your best colour.'

Her face reddened and he perceived a look of hostility, but the animosity in her eyes receded and she shrugged her thin shoulders, smiling bleakly.

'All right,' she said.

She met him at the door when Morgan returned that night. Her hair carried a high sheen from numerous brushings, and she wore a blue sleeveless dress, low cut at the back.

'How do I look?'

'Bloody marvellous,' he said as he took her arm and escorted her to the ancient lift. They caught a taxi to Hillbrow, and he told the driver to stop outside a steakhouse. 'Hungry?' he asked.

'Famished,' Rita assured him.

'We'll eat here and dig the night life later.'

After the meal they walked along the garish neon-lit streets to one of the many discotheques in the district. There, amid the eye-popping psychedelic lights, they danced, drank and listened to the canned music which throbbed around their heads like a thousand demons. At midnight he took her home.

'Enjoyed yourself?' he enquired, in front of her flat.

'Very much. The least I can do is to make you coffee.' They went in and Morgan sprawled tiredly on her bed while she prepared the coffee in the kitchen. She came into the lounge holding two cups. He sat up to take one. She sat down beside him sipping her coffee. Morgan sampled his, found it too hot for his taste and placed it on the floor to cool.

He lay back on the bed and studied her profile as she sipped her coffee. Her appearance was decidedly different from that of the woman he first set eyes on in the waiting room. Suddenly he didn't feel tired anymore. Rita looked around and found him watching her.

'What's on your mind, Roy?'

Morgan continued looking at her with an amused expression on his face. 'You know something?'

'Know what?'

'You're a hell of a sexy bird in that dress.' He stretched out his hand and ran his fingers slowly down her back. 'In fact, you're very desirable when you're not dressed in black.'

He expected Rita to turn hostile. Instead, her eyes twinkled with amusement. She put her coffee down. 'Thanks for the compliment, now what happens?'

'Anything you want.'

She turned her back on Morgan to allow him to unzip her dress. Morgan required little prompting. Rita freed her arms from the dress and rose from the bed. The dress slipped down to her ankles She stepped out of it, facing Morgan in the scantiest of underclothes. He breathed heavily in anticipation.

The laughter had died in her eyes. She fingered her lips nervously as Morgan draped his jacket over the nearest chair. Then she moved towards him, entangling her arms about his waist.

'Damn you,' she whispered in his ear.

Morgan's hands slid over her buttocks as she clung to him. He kissed her and felt her tongue work between his lips and up against his teeth. Her tongue darted in, arousing him to a higher intensity. Their bodies flexed in harmony as they embraced. Suddenly her hands snaked down to his trouser belt. She struggled with the buckle.

'Help me, please help me,' she implored.

He pushed his fingers beneath her hands and unbuckled the belt. Rita dragged his trousers down past his knees in frantic haste. Morgan sat on the edge of the bed and quickly undressed. She knelt between his legs and her lips parted. Morgan clasped the nape of her neck and eased her head down.

He found himself sinking back in erotic delirium, fighting against the temptation of a quick climax. With mental effort he coaxed her up on to the bed beside him. Rita gazed into his eyes. She mustered a faint smile.

'I'm glad you stopped me, Roy,' she murmured. 'After all, we both want satisfying. Don't we?'

She pulled him on top of her.

CHAPTER FIVE

For three months every year, Johannesburg is subjected to a daily thunderstorm. It begins in the late afternoon and usually ends two hours later. On this Sunday, however, the thunderstorm excelled itself. The wispy clouds that started gathering earlier completely fused just before 16:00 hours in a dark grey mantle over the city.

Immediately, as though to order, fierce gusts of wind blew through Johannesburg's grid-patterned streets, sweeping litter before it. Not happy in displaying its strength in the streets, the wind commenced blowing clouds of fine sand off the surrounding goldmine dumps. Then, as the wind reached its peak and intensity, barbed forks of lightning pierced the leaden sky – fingering the dark landscape with flashes. The lightning heralded the first ear-splitting cracks of thunder, reducing the wind to a minor supporting role.

Then the rain came.

It came with a vengeance – crashing down in one continuous downpour, pinning the flying litter to the hissing streets.

Within minutes, the swirling water in the gutters rose and spread across the pavements. Bream and Morgan, heads buried deep inside the upturned collars of their raincoats, splashed their way to the airport bus. The time was 18:45 hours, and the rain gave no indication of ceasing its watery barrage.

They boarded the bus and settled back in the damp warmth for the hour-long drive to Jan Smuts Airport. Bream was seated next to a window. He brushed away the condensation on the glass to allow himself a blurred last view of Johannesburg for the next six months. He wondered if it would indeed be his last view of the city. Morgan offered him a cigarette. Bream gratefully took it.

The rain slackened noticeably as the bus passed through the industrial area of Isando. It petered out completely when they entered the airport gates. The bus drew in on the forecourt of the main terminal and the passengers alighted to collect their luggage from the boot. Bream and Morgan had taken their small holdalls into the bus and had no need to queue for their luggage. Consequently, they walked straight through terminal entrance and into the spacious airport lounge.

Bream was staggered to find it so full. Every chair was occupied and, among the people in the lounge, he saw the odd figure dressed in the jungle-green uniform of 5 Commando. There were also youths with relatives, friends or sweethearts, standing in small groups trying to drum up casual conversation while waiting for the midnight plane. Other men with their wives talked awkwardly beneath the harsh glare of the lounge lights. Passengers waiting for flights to less dangerous places just sat, their eyes filled with unembarrassed curiosity as they stared at the men bound for the Congo. Bream, rather overwhelmed by the circumstances, simply stared back.

Morgan tapped him on the shoulder, interrupting his thoughts. 'Let's go over to the bar and punish a cold lager.'

'I'd prefer a stiff brandy,' replied Bream.

'Come on then, while there's still time. By the way Tim, how many cigarettes have you got?'

'A couple of packets, why?'

'Do yourself a favour and buy as many as you can afford.'

'Good grief! Are cigarettes in short supply up there?'

'It's been known to happen,' Morgan chuckled. 'You needn't worry about paying customs duty. We go through the back door.'

They drifted towards the small bar, pushing their way through the crowd. Morgan ordered the drinks while Bream purchased his cigarettes. Morgan left his friend's brandy on the bar and sipped his lager. Bream joined him.

'When do we get our plane tickets?' he asked.

'When the bloke arrives with them,' came the ambiguous answer. Bream felt Morgan's elbow in his ribs. 'Better finish your drink, Tim. I think he's coming in now.'

CHAPTER FIVE

A ruddy-faced man in his early thirties ambled into the airport lounge, swinging a bulging briefcase. He made a beeline for the bar, halting just a few feet from Bream and Morgan. He unstrapped his briefcase and brought out a large sheet of paper. Men drifted towards him as though drawn by some unspoken command. Bream gulped back his brandy to join the group with Morgan.

'Okay, okay! Give me some air,' beseeched the man.

A married couple, having no interest in the proceedings, moved away and the man dropped his bulky frame in one of the two vacant chairs. He studied the sheet of paper in his hand before scrutinising the men around him.

'Where's the rest? I've got forty names on this list.' He waved the sheet of paper.

'The others didn't see you arrive, that's all,' someone said.

'Do me a favour, pal. Round 'em up,' he begged.

'Only forty here?' broke in Morgan with mock amazement. Don't tell me there's spare seats on the aircraft!'

A burst of laughter greeted his remark.

'That'll be the day,' came the reply. 'There should be some bodies already aboard. The plane calls at Durban before flying on to here.'

The group swelled appreciably as more interested parties gathered around the ruddy-faced man. 'Right,' he said loudly, peering at his sheet of paper. 'Answer when I call your name. Ames?'

'Here!' shouted a man from the back of the crowd.

'Arlington?'

'Here!'

He ticked off each name with a stubby pencil. With profound relief he called out the last name, gratefully placing a tick beside it.

'Anyone present whose name isn't down here? No? Thank God for that!' He folded the list and shoved it in his pocket. 'Now that was thirsty work,' he said. 'So how about, someone buying me a cold beer?'

'You're on a good number, Harry,' declared a uniformed mercenary handing him an opened bottle. 'I wouldn't mind your job in the Jo'burg office. Money for jam.'

The man named Harry grinned openly. 'Get a couple of bullets in you and then apply. That's the way I did it.' He pushed back the cuff of his sleeve and checked his watch. 'There's still time to go, so why don't you boys disperse until the plane arrives?'

The group thinned out and Bream and Morgan returned to the bar. While ordering the drinks, Bream noticed Ashton quietly sipping a large pink gin at the far end of the bar. Although bound for a war, Toby Ashton looked the impeccable Englishman. He wore a double-breasted black sports jacket with shiny brass buttons and, around his neck, was a paisley patterned cravat – the ends neatly tucked into a white open-necked shirt. His grey worsted trousers, sharply pressed, angled down to his gleaming shoes. In all respects, his attire suggested a holiday mood.

'I'm sure I saw that guy in the waiting room on our first visit to the recruiting office,' whispered Bream, handing his friend a lager.

Morgan followed Bream's gaze.

'If he thinks he's going to a game of tennis, I've got news for him,' said Morgan with a laugh. He drank his lager and plonked his glass on the bar counter. 'Come on,' he said, 'let's go and eat.'

They went upstairs to the self-service restaurant. On their return to the airport lounge they observed the man called Harry telling everybody to gather around him again.

'Okay, you guys,' he bawled, clasping a bunch of air tickets. 'Forty of you here are going north, but only thirty will make it back! That's a statistic based on former contracts. So, if anyone wants to dip out, now's his chance.'

'What about the boys flying in from Durban?' interjected a voice.

Harry smiled benignly at his questioner. 'They'll be staying on board until the plane takes off again. I'm just, telling you how many will be returning from the guys here.' He peered at the sea of faces. 'Well?' he inquired. Nobody moved. 'Right. When you've got your ticket, go straight to customs. Now where is Ames?'

'Here I am,' called a thin youth.

'Catch!'

Harry flicked an air ticket, in Ames's direction.

'Arlington?'

Arlington, positioned in front of Harry, simply held out his hand. Bream grunted a reply when his name was called and grasped his air ticket firmly. He slipped it inside his passport, picked up his holdall and went through the barrier to customs. There, his passport was checked but not stamped. He then continued into the in-transit lounge, seating himself on one of the long wooden benches, waiting for Morgan to appear.

The benches were more than half full by the time Morgan arrived. He had just seated himself next to Bream when a DC4 rumbled out of the darkness and on to the tarmac apron in front of the in-transit lounge windows.

The aircraft was, judging by its markings, on charter from Trans Air Africa, a Rhodesian air company.

When all had passed through customs, an officer in the dark blue uniform of Trans Air Africa entered the lounge. He stood for a few seconds, surveying his passengers with a whimsical smile. He watched them fidgeting, waiting for his word which would send them grabbing for their meagre luggage, jostling each other through the door, trying to get the best seats on the aircraft.

'Well?' he said quietly. 'Who's for the Congo?'

CHAPTER SIX

Colin Fletcher gritted his teeth as the hotted-up Citroen's front wheels left the rutted surface of the dirt road. Two breathless seconds later the car hit the far edge of a deep pothole. The driver coolly brought the bucking vehicle under control without slackening speed.

Fortunately, Fletcher was wedged tightly between two of his fellow aircraft mechanics, otherwise he felt, sure that his head would have come into forcible contact with the roof.

'Watch it, Carlos!' he yelled, admonishing the swarthy-skinned driver in the grey flying suit. 'Every time you drive this motorised junk to the airport, you always hit that bloody hole!'

Carlos Garrity glanced into the rearview mirror and grinned wickedly at Fletcher. 'It's the best way I know of shaking off hangovers. Lots of speed means much fresh air. And fresh air clears my head of last night's whisky fumes. Do you not agree, Max?' said Garrity, loudly addressing the tired young man on Fletcher's left.

Max Gehlen was of the same nationality as the fair-haired man sitting on Fletcher's right. Both Germans – and at five in the morning, very sleepy Germans.

Fletcher had Gehlen's sympathy. It was bad enough getting up at 4 am after a long night of drinking, but ten times worse being driven along a typical Congo road by a mad Cuban at a speed defying gravity.

'No, I don't agree,' replied Gehlen in a sour tone. 'I wish you would wind up your window too. We're slowly freezing to death back here.'

The road from Albertville to the airport ran along the coast. Garrity cast a look at the heaving waters of Lake Tanganyika.

He smiled to himself. Gehlen was right about the fresh air. There was a veritable wind coming off the lake, rolling up the normally placid waters into foam-topped waves which surged against the sandy shore. The sky appeared ominous too. A thick blanket of cloud hung low across the horizon, blotting out the pale distant mountains on the Tanzanian side of the lake.

The sky above was also cloudy. Garrity hoped that the clouds wouldn't descend any lower, otherwise his dawn sortie might be in danger of being cancelled. He loved flying. It was his life. He had been a pilot in the Cuban Air Force until Fidel Castro ousted Batista. Shortly afterwards Garrity found it prudent to escape to the United States where he obtained employment as a crop-spraying pilot in Alabama.

He was in the job for just a year when the Central Intelligence Agency discreetly approached him to partake in the abortive Bay of Pigs invasion. Garrity was given a B26 to fly – without guns. Then they gave him guns but took away his armament of bombs and rockets. He lost count of what he could and couldn't use after that. What with the swapping of weapons and the changing of targets, he wasn't at all surprised to find himself on the losing side.

Now, thanks to an obscure department of the CIA, he was again flying an obsolete B26 and getting paid handsomely for his troubles. He was even paid overtime rates when the occasion called for it, much to his amusement. In this war, however, his B26 was magnificently armed with clusters of two-inch rockets and eight .50 calibre machine guns.

Sometimes though, he yearned for the napalm bombs which he knew were close at hand but which he was forbidden to carry because of political reasons. If anything could bring this savage war to an end, reflected Garrity, it would be napalm bombs. The Simbas would capitulate within weeks.

Garrity reduced speed on approaching the narrow bridge which spanned a large estuary on the outskirts of Albertville. The bridge was the vital link between Albertville and the airport and was guarded around the clock. He waved to the four Congolese soldiers sitting in a machine gun emplacement before pressing his foot hard down on the accelerator pedal to beat an ANC truck approaching from the other side.

The driver pulled over onto the verge when he saw the Citroen race onto the bridge. The Cuban pilot cheekily honked the horn as he drove past the truck. The road forked sharply at the end of the bridge. Fletcher closed his eyes as the car tyres screeched in protest. Garrity, with superb aplomb, skilfully brought the Citroen under control.

Fletcher opened his eyes as they flew past a ruined Texaco service station that could only be about six years old, but was now devoid of pumps and forecourt. Encroaching grass and weeds had churned up the forecourt while elephant grass, five feet high, grew abundantly around the rusting metal pole that held the Texaco sign. Not a pane of glass lay intact in the service station's windows, and the once white walls were liberally pockmarked with bullet holes.

Fletcher had to pass the service station every working day, but it never failed to amaze him. To him, it was a constant, example of the Congo's independence. He was glad that he had only five months left of his one-year contract.

Born in 1942, Fletcher had always lived in his hometown of Nottingham. He was schooled there and began work at the nearby Saunders-Roe aircraft factory as an apprentice aircraft mechanic. He eventually became a fully-fledged tradesman and rather settled in his work when he noticed many of his friends resigning from their jobs for greener pastures abroad. Suddenly, he too felt the urge to see something of the world.

His chance came when a rumour swept through the factory that a company called WIGMO was recruiting trained aircraftsmen for the Congo. Fletcher had only heard of the country from newspaper reports, but when he heard of the high wages WIGMO were prepared to pay, his curiosity knew no bounds.

He applied for an interview. A week later he was asked to travel down to London with a view to see whether he would be suitable for a position. Upon arriving at WIGMO's London office, Fletcher discovered to his amusement that the company was registered in Lichtenstein. He also discovered that his salary, when working in the Congo, would be paid in American dollars into any bank in the world wherever he chose to have an account.

WIGMO would also pay him ten thousand Congolese francs weekly for living expenses. His tour of duty would be a full year with an option for a further year's contract should he desire it. They stipulated that he would have to pay his own air fare to the Congo which would be reimbursed on completion of his contract. At that time, they would also pay his air fare home.

In fairness, WIGMO warned Fletcher that the standard of living in the Congo was not that of England. Moreover, it, was possible that he would find himself servicing planes in what was termed a 'danger zone'. But that was the principal reason why the company paid their employees such high salaries.

They failed to mention, however, that Fletcher's superiors above airport manager level were not Congolese as he imagined, but American. Nor was it mentioned that ten thousand Congolese francs, once worth £20, barely fetched £20 on the black market.

Fletcher ran his fingers through his unruly hair. It seemed years since he last saw Nottingham. The airport, loomed ghostlike in the grey dawn. His bleary eyes took in the three bleak shapes of the twin-engine B26s, drawn up in close proximity to the small control building. He yawned in a dispirited fashion as Garrity drove the car through the guarded entrance. Another twelve-hour working day was about to commence.

Garrity parked by a large wooden shed on the left side of the entrance. He turned to his three passengers. 'Move your arses,' he said cheerfully. 'We've arrived.'

'Thanks to a miracle – yes,' grumbled Gehlen, opening the door on his side.

Fletcher followed Gehlen out of the car, leaving Gehlen's fellow countryman to slide out the other side. Fletcher flexed his arms and stamped his feet vigorously on the ground, attempting to shake off his tiredness.

A Volkswagen Kombi was stationary near the three B26s. Fletcher glimpsed the lanky figure of Jim Oakly, the airport manager, disappearing behind the Kombi. Fletcher knew him from Saunders-Roe, being another volunteer exile from the British aircraft industry. He came into view at the back of the vehicle and signalled to Fletcher to join him.

He stood beneath the cockpit of the nearest B26 when Fletcher reached him. Behind Oakly, and painted vividly on the B26's dark fuselage, was a large red-and-black cartoon painting of a wild-eyed bull, with the word 'Makasi' written below it.

The same picture of the bull adorned every aircraft that came under WIGMO's jurisdiction. It originated in the early part of the war when an employee decided, in an alcoholic state, that WIGMO should have an insignia. An equally drunken colleague suggested the fiery bull which appeared on the label of a well-known Congo beer. His suggestion was carried unanimously. The subsequent fame of the Makasi bull spread right across the Congo. The insignia even appeared printed on the fronts of t-shirts. Albertville's Palace Hotel too, which WIGMO acquisitioned for exclusive use of their staff, was known locally as the Makasi Club. Thanks to aircraft arriving at Albertville Airport from every corner of the country, the Makasi Club stocked an enviable selection of drink.

Fletcher watched Oakly rub his prominent jaw. It was a habit of the airport manager when in a pensive mood.

'We've got a spot of trouble with this Bravo's port engine,' he said in a broad Yorkshire accent, using the codename given to all B26 aircraft. 'Now take the Kombi and drive over to the Tangos where you'll find Gerald Weston. Get him in the Kombi with his tools and drive back here. Don't waste any time as I've got a job for you on another Bravo.'

Fletcher climbed into the Kombi and motored along the runway towards six ancient T-28 fighter aircraft, drawn up in line on the far side of the airport. He found Weston sitting in a cockpit, tinkering with the controls.

'The old man wants you in a hurry with your tools.'

Weston leaned over the side of the cockpit and frowned at Fletcher. 'What's the flap?' he asked.

'Something's wrong with the port engine of Carlos's Bravo.'

'Couldn't you fix it?' queried Weston.

'Probably, but Jim's got another job for me,' replied Fletcher.

'This whole air force is falling apart if you ask me,' said Weston, easing his body from the cockpit.

'I don't have to,' said Fletcher with a grin, familiar with Weston's favourite topic. They walked to the Kombi and Fletcher started driving back to the B26s.

'Do you know that only three of those Tangos are airworthy,' persisted Weston. 'If we don't get spares soon, we'll be forced to cannibalise from one of the others. Those damned Cubans don't help much to keep them airworthy either. You know what I found stuck in the landing gear of one yesterday? Half a bloody palm tree! Talk about low flying. I'm waiting for the day when I find some poor bloody rebel impaled on the end of one of the machine-gun barrels. It can't be too far away,' he added sourly.

'Speaking of rebels, Gerald, when is this plane load of mercenaries due in?'

Weston glanced at his wristwatch. '19:30 I think.' He pulled a face. 'Bang goes our lovely beer supply at the club.'

Fletcher laughed. 'I'd much rather have them around than that mob,' he said, jerking a thumb at two rows of khaki tents, ringed with sand-filled oil drums.

Weston cast a sardonic eye at four Congolese soldiers visible behind the oil drums.

'You could be right about that,' he said.

CHAPTER SEVEN

In the backyard shed of 5 Commando's Albertville headquarters, a Congolese youth studiously put in the last crease in Sergeant Brogan's jungle green shirt. He has been hard at work an hour before dawn, preparing Brogan's kit for the coming day. He placed the ancient coal iron on the concrete floor and snuffed out a flickering candle. It was now sufficiently light to see without it.

He picked up the shirt and slipped on the red epaulettes with the single silver star which denoted that his master was the Provost Sergeant of 5 Commando's military police. He folded the shirt and laid it on a pair of immaculately pressed jungle green trousers, after which he ran a critical eye over Brogan's polished combat boots and the freshly-blancoed webbing, hanging over a line in the shed to dry. After he felt certain that Brogan couldn't find fault with his work, the youth went to a hissing primus stove near the doorway.

On top of the stove was an enamel saucepan, holding water for Brogan's shave and also for his habitual morning coffee. The water was coming to the boil. He fetched a tin mug from a shelf and spooned in a large amount of coffee. By that time the water was boiling well. He took the saucepan and filled the mug, stirring vigorously at the same time. It was too strong for him, but not for Brogan. Sergeant Brogan preferred his coffee like his women. Hot and black.

After replacing the saucepan on the primus stove, he picked up the mug of coffee and walked gingerly to the rear door of the headquarters which, before the rebellion, was the local cinema. The youth walked past the radio operator's room, turned right into an empty room, walked through the door at the end and turned right again. There, in front of him, was Brogan's room. He did not knock, but pushed open the door and tiptoed across to the sergeant's bedside locker, where he carefully set down the coffee.

Brogan's kit boy peered through the mosquito net at the bulbous naked body. Brogan lay flat on his back, his mouth open with his huge stomach rising and falling in phase with his snores. A discarded brandy bottle lay on its side beside the uncommonly high bed. It was a comfortable bed, unlike the stretcher variety from the commando stores. Brogan had commandeered it from Albertville Hospital during his first contract in the Congo.

The youth hesitantly raised the mosquito net and shook Brogan's right ankle. Incoherent noises emitted from his open mouth, followed by slurred swearing as Brogan slowly awakened from his drunken sleep. Brogan's obscene mutterings had little effect on the youth. It was part of the early morning ritual. Like the coffee, hot shaving water, and the evidence about the room of a drunken evening.

Brogan rubbed his eyelids with the back of his hand and glared at his kit boy.

'Bonjour, Mon Adjutant,' said the youth politely.

'Balls,' said Brogan, groping for a packet of cigarettes.

His kit boy backed out through the door. After much fumbling he found his cigarettes and lit one before flopping back on the mattress, scratching at the jungle of hair on his chest with stubby fingers. He lay there for some time, the cigarette clamped between his blubbery lips. Suddenly Brogan sat up and threw back the mosquito net. He took the cigarette from his lips and grasped the handle of the mug with his free hand. He blew noisily on the coffee and sipped hurriedly, before stretching himself out again, smoking.

Sergeant Brogan was a forty-five-year-old bachelor by choice and traveller by nature. He was born in a Montreal backstreet tenement building of a French mother and Irish father. He spoke both English and French fluently by the time he went to school, but that was about the limit of Brogan's education.

He'd rather spend his days down at the docks on the St Lawrence Seaway than in the schoolroom at the bottom of the street. His parents weren't worried either. He'd been a mistake in any case.

Brogan was conceived on a bitterly cold night when they were both drunk. They didn't want him, and they made him know it. Not surprisingly the feeling became mutual over the years. In his early teens, Brogan went to the docks and shipped out on a tramp steamer. And that was the last time he saw home.

Brogan first heard about the Congo mercenaries when his ship called in to Durban. There he saw wads of banknotes being flashed around the city's fleshpots by men who had returned from the Congo.

He was impressed. Brogan duly arrived in the Congo and discovered that a mercenary's life was far harder than he had imagined.

Brogan looked around and saw that life was a good deal easier as a military policeman. He immediately applied to be one. The commanding officer was out of the country at the time and Commandant Simon Morley was the acting CO, Brogan's application was accepted without comment.

He was also given the rank of sergeant during the last contract. Now he was on a new contract, and he wondered what changes would affect him during the next six months.

His kit boy returned with his newly pressed uniform. Brogan crushed out the cigarette and finished his coffee. Another day was about to begin. A day of sorting out recruits and being stared at by returning mercenaries. He wasn't looking forward to it. Then he brightened up. After all, it could be a profitable day.

High above Albertville the Trans Air Africa Dakota dipped through a heavy bank of cloud. From his seat, Bream saw the dark green mountains at the back of Albertville. He also saw the waters of Lake Tanganyika lapping whitely along the curling coastline before the aircraft straightened out for the landing.

He leaned back in his seat, feeling awfully muzzy from spending the night half awake. Some of 5 Commando's veterans had vacated their seats during the night for the dubious comfort of the floor. Liberal slugs of liquor had assisted them to sleep for the better part of the journey.

Bream tightened his safety belt and nervously ran his tongue over his dry lips. He glanced at two mercenaries seated across the aisle. Bream was selfishly pleased to see that the nearest one, judging from his expression, was also experiencing the same awesome feeling of journeying into the unknown. The furthest mercenary, a man in his early forties, just stared ahead. His face devoid of all emotion. Morgan frowned good-naturedly at Bream fidgeting in his seat. Bream, on his part, handed back a sick smile and stiffened up in his seat, tensing himself for the landing.

Nobody spoke as the DC4 touched down, its tyres rasping on the tarmac runway. The occupants felt a jolt, when the tailwheel came into contact with the ground and then everybody seemed to breathe in unison. The DC4 continued speeding down the runway, slowing noticeably as the small airport buildings came into view on the port side. The pilot brought the aircraft on to the concrete apron next to the three B26s and cut out the engines. At that exact moment the two powerful engines of the nearest B26 burst into life. The mercenaries watched the B26 growl onto the same runway which their DC4 had just occupied, and subconsciously identified themselves with the B26 as it rumbled along, in readiness for take-off.

Bream's wide eyes followed the path of the aircraft, and he tried to guess its destination. His first visit to a battle zone, and the scholar within Bream wanted to digest everything that could affect him in the month to come. Morgan noted his vivid curiosity.

'Probably going on a dawn patrol to Baraka,' he said helpfully 'It's a nice feeling to see old Bravo circling overhead when you're in trouble.'

Bream checked his watch. 'A bit, late for a dawn patrol, isn't it?'

'Everything has a habit of being late in the Congo. Including pay.'

The Trans Air Africa officer who had told them to board the aircraft at Jan Smuts Airport came into the passenger compartment. He went to the hatch and unlocked it. A welcome flow of fresh air entered the DC4 as he opened the hatch. Mercenaries levered themselves from their seats, flexing their cramped limbs, gathering up their cabin luggage. Nobody, however, was particularly keen to be the first out.

'Come on!' urged an anonymous voice from the back of the aircraft. 'Doesn't anyone want to go to war?'

There came a short burst of ironical laughter, mostly from men who had made the trip before. The pointed question had an effect though, and a general exodus from the DC4 began.

Morgan smothered a grin as he watched his friend descend awkwardly to the ground. The conventional type of steps that passengers use on civilian airports simply did not exist at Albertville Airport. The way down was by means of a perpendicular ladder. A group of Congolese labourers started shifting the bulkier luggage from the DC4's cargo hold and loading it on to a battered blue truck which had reversed up to the aircraft. Two 5 Commando policemen, their white webbing gleaming immaculately over their jungle-green uniforms, shepherded the mercenaries to the large wooden shed on the airport perimeter. Morgan hovered close to Bream like a big protective brother.

'Don't ever get tangled up with that bastard,' he said in a low voice, nodding towards the unconcerned figure of Sergeant Brogan.

Bream cautiously observed Brogan tapping his right thigh with an ivory-tipped baton, watching the last few mercenaries hurry into the shed.

'Why? Who the hell is he?' asked Bream, feeling edgy.

'That's Brogan, Sergeant Frenchie Brogan. Mean as a snake and Congo happy. Nothing pleases him more than giving guys a hard time, so watch your step when he's around,' warned Morgan.

'Thanks for the advice.'

'It's the least I can do. I'd warn my worst enemy about that bastard,' grunted Morgan stonily.

Brogan turned and faced the mercenaries. 'A couple of trucks will be arriving soon to take your bodies to HQ.' Brogan paused and studied the host of new volunteers in the group. 'No doubt there are some of you who've got South African or Rhodesian currency, maybe a few English pounds as well. Now when you think about it, there ain't much you can do with that sort of currency in this beat-up country.' He paused again, allowing time for his words to sink home. Then he coughed loudly and began walking up and down in front of them.

Morgan prodded Bream in the ribs.

'Here comes the blarney,' he whispered.

'Now if you can't spend it here, you'll want to get rid of it and I'm the man to help you.' Brogan patted his left breast pocket. 'I've got on me a few – just a few, mind you – a few thousand Congolese francs. All legal tender here, not like your foreign currency.'

'So fucking what,' mouthed Morgan.

'Now this is your chance of converting your foreign currency into francs at the rate of two rands a thousand.' Brogan said dramatically, peering at the recruits. 'The official exchange is two rand for five hundred francs, so you're getting a bargain. And the reason why you're getting a bargain is because lads who've finished their contracts sold me their surplus francs, so that I can pass the benefit on to you lot. And now I'm doing just that. But I've only got a limited supply, so the first ones get them. Right! Now who are going to be the lucky ones?'

A dozen hands shot up.

'Bloody fools,' muttered a second contract man.

'Stop talking in the ranks!' roared Brogan, the muscles in his fleshy cheeks quivering. 'Any more chat and I'll have you marching to HQ. Luggage and all.'

His voice changed to a kindly tone immediately afterwards as he stalked to the nearest victim, enquiring how much currency the recruit wished to convert. Four other recruits fell for Brogan's glib talk before two army trucks drove through the airport gates.

'Okay! Let's have you,' he bellowed as the trucks pulled up in front of the shed. 'Get on them and fast! There's plenty you guys have got to do today.'

They scrambled aboard the trucks, throwing their kit on before them. Bream braced his legs and gripped the top of the tailboard of the vehicle as it accelerated away without warning. He heard Morgan swear when the driver turned on to the road at speed, pitching Morgan and other mercenaries to the floorboards.

Brogan with the other MP were out in front in a jeep. The jeep, unlike the two trucks, took the uneven road in its stride.

Congolese women, colourfully dressed, waved at the small convoy as it sped towards Albertville. After recovering his breath, Bream began to enjoy the excitement of the trip. Everything he saw enchanted him. The rich redness of the earth, the fresh greenery of the hilly countryside – it was all a new experience. The vast expanse of Lake Tanganyika, however, impressed him most.

'Watch out!' yelled someone.

Everybody in the truck ducked their heads to escape the low foliage of a tree, overhanging the road. Supple, leafy branches dapped against the cab roof, flashing quickly over – the heads of the cowering passengers. One recruit, near the tailboard, wasn't fast enough. He grunted in pain as a slender twig whipped across his face. Bream looked back at the truck behind and saw the mercenaries in that speeding vehicle ducking down as well. Morgan grabbed his shoulder and shouted into his ear.

'That's the cemetery over there.'

Bream glanced towards the right and noticed a low stone wall along the bank. He could see over the wall from his vantage point and was morbidly impressed by the number of steel helmets perched on wooden crosses dotted about the cemetery. He pulled a wry face at Morgan.

A few two-storey houses came into view on each side of the road as the convoy reached the outskirts of Albertville. The houses had obviously been the homes of Europeans, but now were crammed full of Congolese. Bream thought it sad to see such fine buildings in urgent need of repair and the gardens returning to jungle.

Tall palm trees appeared, lining the main street. For a moment Bream thought the convoy was proceeding through Albertville, but the trucks followed Brogan's jeep when it turned to the right up a side road.

Brogan's jeep finally stopped outside a large brown and grey concrete building with windows at ground floor level only. A blue and gold Congolese flag fluttered weakly on a wooden pole near the path leading to the building.

'5 Commando HQ,' said Morgan to Bream. 'This is where we disembark.'

He was right. Brogan climbed out of his jeep and walked back to the now stationary trucks. He strode between the vehicles, smacking the metal sides with his baton.

'Out you get and have a pen ready.'

'What's happening now?' asked Bream.

'More form filling most likely,' said Morgan before jumping to the ground.

A fresh-faced young man in his middle twenties, and sporting two gold stars on his epaulettes, came out of the building. Brogan saluted him. The officer handed Brogan a list of names and then went back inside. Brogan swivel led around and stepped off the path.

'Right, you lot,' he said, addressing them. 'I'm going to call out your names in alphabetical order. When you hear your own name, start lining up by the side door. Now listen carefully, because if you don't you won't be paid. Okay, let's go. Ames! Arlington! Ashton! Ayres!'

He barked out each name with machine-gun precision. Bream's name soon came, and he joined the queue. The other MP who did not have a silver star on his red epaulettes held the door open, allowing one person into the building at a time. When Bream headed the queue, the MP pointed across the expansive interior where he glimpsed the man before him disappearing into another room.

'When he comes out, you go in,' said the MP.

The recruit reappeared within a minute, grasping a fistful of Congolese banknotes. Bream walked through and found two mercenaries seated at a long table.

'Name?' enquired one, a copy of Brogan's sheet in front of him.

'Bream.'

His name was ticked, and thirty thousand francs was presented to him. Bream stuffed the notes in his hip pocket and walked back through the large room. The room was rectangular in shape with the painted remains of a cinema screen on the furthest wall. He came out of the door and spotted Morgan in the queue. He stopped and grinned, not realising that Brogan was looking at him.

'You there!' yelled Brogan. 'Don't hang about like an unpaid tart. Get over to the cookhouse and report back here when you've eaten.'

'Christ!' muttered Bream, wending his way to a bungalow which the man before him had just entered.

He was served with a mess tin of tea without milk or sugar and handed a thick slab of bread with scrambled egg piled on it. He sat down at a crowded table and sank his teeth into the bread and scrambled egg. The first taste informed him that the bread was stale, and the egg was powdered egg. It was then he felt the first twinge of homesickness. Another recruit squeezed in opposite him. He was the same person whom Bream had seen on the aircraft across the aisle from him. His features no longer held a wooden countenance which Bream had noticed when the DC4 circled above Albertville Airport. Instead, his face wore an exceptionally morose expression. Bream took comfort in the fact that even older men than himself seemed to suffer from bouts of homesickness.

The cookhouse was decidedly overcrowded by the time Morgan arrived. Bream hurriedly drank most of his black tea and vacated his seat for his friend to sit down.

He moved through the men sitting on the steps and on the grass outside the cookhouse. They had given up the struggle of finding space inside. He continued on to the narrow muddy road and wandered back to the old cinema. There, he joined the other recruits who had also finished their meal. Seconds later, the strutting figure of Brogan rounded the bend some forty yards away.

'You recruits,' he shouted. 'There's been a change in plans, and I want you all formed up in columns of two on the road, so move!'

Bream and his companions scampered on to the road and lined up two abreast, waiting for Brogan's next order. 'You're to be kitted out, so I'm gonna call you to attention and march you down to stores.' Brogan stepped back and surveyed them from the road verge. 'Stand properly at ease and wait for my command. Squad!' The recruit next to Bream immediately came to attention. Brogan stared at him in mock despair and then walked up to the man. 'What's your name, soldier?'

'Dryden, Sergeant.'

'Dryden,' rejoined Brogan heavily. 'Don't anticipate my commands.' Dryden shrugged his shoulders. 'Okay,' he said.

Before he knew what was happening, Brogan grabbed him by his shirt front. 'I've a rank, Dryden. A rank! I've also got the authority to have you doubling up and down this road until you drop. If that doesn't cure you, I've got something else. Up there! Up there behind that hill in front of your beady eyes, Dryden. It's a Congolese jail, Dryden. Full of kaffirs stinking the place out. And if I get any more insolence from you, my lad, that's where you'll spend the night. Understand?' Brogan relaxed his grip and pushed Dryden back into line. 'All right, everyone stand at ease. Squad! Attention! Move to the right in column of twos – right turn! By the right – quick march.'

They marched around the corner and over the concrete forecourt of a defunct service station, then back on to Albertville's main street – a dirt road with open sewers on either side. Congolese tailors on the sidewalk, huddled over their sewing machines, looked up briefly to see them march by. Ebony-skinned women with babies wrapped securely on their backs stopped gossiping in the dark stores and flashed smiles at them.

Brogan halted the column in front of a long one-storey type of warehouse. He made them get into single file before ordering them in. One at a time they went up to a small counter and were given a kitbag, already packed, and a pair of boots. When everybody had been kitted out, Brogan formed them up on the road again and marched them back to the old cinema. There, he told them to fall out and place their newly acquired army kit with the rest of their belongings. Bream lit a cigarette to calm his swimming head as Brogan collected another party for the march to stores.

Morgan was among the last group to return. He thankfully slung his kitbag and boots down by Bream's kit.

'Bit of a change from Jo'burg, isn't it Tim?' he said cheerfully.

'Dead right it is,' remarked Bream, eyeing the heavy combat boots by his own kitbag and then at the lightweight shoes on his feet. At that moment Brogan and the officer, he was with at the pay parade walked out of 5 Commando headquarters.

'Leave your kit and form three ranks across the road,' ordered Brogan, gesturing with his baton. 'Lieutenant Radcliffe wants a word with you.'

They quickly sorted themselves out, into three ranks and, with Brogan hovering in the background, they waited for the officer to speak.

'Stand easy and listen to what I have to say,' the officer said. 'The sergeant's just told you my name and I'm in charge of Base HQ, known to some of you from previous contracts as Paradise. That being the call sign. I am also responsible for what you do in this town. So, listen to me good and hard if you want to stay out of trouble.'

'Tonight – I repeat, tonight – the town is out of bounds to everyone except the base staff. And if anyone thinks he's clever enough to go into town he will have Sergeant Brogan to reckon with. You'll be free to go in tomorrow night, but don't get too drunk in the shebeens if you must drink. Whether you're drunk or not, watch your step if you visit Casper's. That place spells trouble. You men who know Albertville had better wise-up the new boys to the whereabouts of Casper's. In any case, there are better places to have a quiet drink. Like the Hotel du Lac or the Makasi Club at the Palace Hotel.

'Take my tip and have as little to do as possible with the Congolese. Above all, keep away from their women. The same rules apply here as in South Africa, whatever your nationality.'

Radcliffe noted the wide grins on some of the faces. 'Oh, sure you can smile and laugh, but from experience I know that the worst offenders are South Africans.' The grins vanished.

'So, remember that Albertville isn't Lourenco Marques. I am warning you, too, that if you're caught having a bit of tail with a native woman, you'll be slapped straight into the Box. And it isn't pleasant. We call the local Congolese jail the Box, and if you're unfortunate enough to be locked in it you'll understand why we call it the Box. What's more you only get fed when someone down here thinks of it. The Congolese guards have strict orders not to feed any 5 Commando prisoners.

'Now a word about your living quarters. Until you go to Baraka you'll be staying in the bungalows next to the cookhouse. You won't find any furniture in them, but the floors are reasonably clean and there's some stretchers in HQ stores.

'It's a question, however, of first come first served. Make sure there's always someone guarding your kit in the bungalows, because the Congolese kids around here will have it away in no time at all if you don't.

'While the CO is away 5 Commando comes under the control Of Commandant Morley. We're expecting him shortly and he's a stickler for discipline, so don't let him catch any of you unshaven or slouching around like refugees from the ANC.

'When I've finished talking, I want you all to queue up outside HQ and come inside six at a time, where you'll sign your official contracts. When you've done that, take your kit up to the bungalows and change into uniform. Then pack up your civvies and deposit them in the stores.' Radcliffe looked briefly at Brogan. 'That's all. Carry on, Sergeant.'

'Very good sir,' said Brogan stiffly, saluting Radcliffe. Radcliffe returned his salute and walked back into the building. Brogan clicked his fingers at the first man in the front rank. 'Start going across. The rest of you follow on.'

Bream was in the front rank and soon found himself in the large hall that had once been the cinema. Three uniformed mercenaries sat behind desks which, judging from the design, had been acquired from a school. He was directed to the most distant desk where he was given three contracts to complete and sign in triplicate.

They were written in French, but the mercenary at the desk assisted him. Brogan walked over to Bream just as he signed the last copy.

'You look like you've got a bit of grey matter up here,' began Brogan, tapping his forehead. 'What's your name?'

'Bream, Sergeant,' he replied, remembering the unfortunate recruit who had omitted Brogan's rank.

'There's a small table in the next room, Bream. Bring it out here and get yourself a chair, because you're going to help out. Otherwise, we'll be here not only for the rest of the day, but half the night as well. Volunteer McKay here will give you some contracts.'

Bream carried the small desk from the other room and put it down next to McKay's desk. He saw a chair at the back of the hall and, while he fetched it, McKay stacked a pile of contracts on the table.

'Don't be afraid to ask me any questions if you get stuck,' he informed Bream as Brogan sent a recruit to Bream's table. Much to Bream's interest the recruit was the man who looked so homesick in the cookhouse.

'Name?' asked Bream, his pen poised above the top contract.

'Marralich. Louis Hendrick Marralich.'

He wrote the name in the appropriate places on all three contracts before turning the contracts in Marralich's direction.

Bream pointed his finger at some wording. 'This line says whether you're single, separated, married or divorced. You delete the ones which aren't applicable.'

He watched Marralich cross out every word except divorce. Bream moved his finger down to the next line. 'Now write your age, next-of-kin etcetera, etcetera. Do the same on the copies.'

Marralich carefully complied with Bream's instructions until only one page on each contract need to be completed.

'This page is the will,' explained Bream. 'On this line you write in the person's name you want the insurance money to go to should you die up here. Then write in the beneficiary's address on the next line and sign your name below it.' Marralich wrote the name in block capitals, drew a dash and added 'daughter', after which he filled in the address and quickly signed all three contracts.

Marralich straightened up, pocketed his pen and gazed critically at Bream. 'Is that all?' He gave a soft, unsteady laugh. 'Or to be more precise, am I now a fully-fledged member of 5 Commando?'

'That's about it, I reckon,' answered Bream.

'Good,' said Marralich with deep satisfaction.

He walked away and Brogan sent another recruit to Bream. In all he helped over a dozen men to complete their contracts before Brogan detailed someone else to relieve him. Bream collected his kit and staggered up to the bungalows. He heard Morgan call his name as he passed the first bungalow. He looked and saw Morgan waving to him from a front window.

'In here, Tim,' he shouted. 'I've reserved a space for you.'

Morgan took the heavy kitbag from him on entering the bungalow and pushed him into the front room. Judging from the number of men and the amount of kit, in the room, Bream gathered that he would be sharing it with at least eight others.

'Crowded, but it's only for a couple of days,' stated Morgan. 'I heard on the grapevine that the *Rachelle* sails for Baraka shortly.'

'*Rachelle*?'

'It's a motorised barge. Crawls along at snail's pace,' he said with a sniff. 'Haven't been on it, but the boys who have tell me it's a right bastard.'

A folded stretcher stood against the wall by Bream's kit. 'Whose is that?' he asked.

'Yours,' Morgan told him. 'I managed to bring back two from stores. You'd better unstrap it quick before someone takes a fancy to it.'

'Thanks for getting it. This floor does look a bit hard.' confessed Bream.

At 5 Commando HQ, Brogan stomped up and down the large hall, haranguing the last four recruits to hurry. They completed their contracts under a verbal stream of abuse and gladly vacated the premises. Radcliffe approached Brogan and pointed to his watch.

'I suggest you get down to the Hotel du Lac as soon as you can Sergeant,' he said worriedly. 'It won't do to keep Commandant Morley waiting.'

'I'm on my way right now,' announced Brogan, heading for the door.

He got into his jeep and started the engine. He noticed Radcliffe panicking a bit, as he drove off. And Brogan knew why.

Radcliffe was scared of the commandant. Nothing really unusual as Morley was capable of scaring anybody. With Radcliffe, however, it was something more. On occasions he acted like an animated puppet when Morley was around. It was more than a question of *yes sir, no sir, three bags full, sir*. Much more, but Brogan couldn't put his finger on the root cause. He could only surmise that Morley had some kind of hold over Radcliffe. Although he hadn't discussed the point with the base staff – they thought Radcliffe was just sucking up to Morley – Brogan would dearly love a second opinion. He hated loose ends, but if he asked Radcliffe personally about his observations the lieutenant might jump the other way. A move that could lead to his downfall. Mindful of this danger, Brogan suppressed his curiosity and kept his observations to himself.

Hotel du Lac where Morley was staying was considered to be the best hotel in Albertville since the more modern one, Palace Hotel, was taken over lock, stock and barrel by WIGMO. Before Independence the Hotel du Lac had catered for the higher income European who spent his vacation in the once popular lakeside resort of Albertville. Those balmy days had receded violently into the colonial past, but the hotel stubbornly strived to keep some traces of its former glory. Belgian Army officers and the majority of the American military advisers, including members of the CIA attached to Operations-South Headquarters, stayed there. Officers of 5 Commando, who could easily afford the hotel's tariff, also made a point of staying there. Not unnaturally, so did Commandant Simon Morley.

Brogan spotted the commandant standing on the steps when he was still some way off. He stood alone, looking to Brogan like some latter-day Napoleon, but twice as aloof. Brogan pulled in by the hotel steps, alighted from the jeep and saluted Morley. The commandant descended to the sidewalk before reciprocating Brogan's salute.

'For a moment I thought you were going to be late, Sergeant,' said Morley, displaying a smile that displayed his teeth like ivory icicles.

Brogan had been fooled by that peculiar expression once before. And once was enough. Now he only smiled back when he was absolutely sure that Morley was being humorous. Out there, in front of the hotel, Brogan had his doubts. He decided to err on the side of caution.

'I always try to be prompt, sir,' he replied attentively.

'Keep it that way and we'll get along fine, Sergeant,' said Morley, walking briskly around the jeep and climbing into the passenger seat. Sergeant Brogan scrambled back behind the wheel, did a jerky three-point turn in the street, and headed back to Base HQ.

'Any problems with the new intake?' asked Morley.

'Not yet, sir. They've all been kitted out and documented,' responded Brogan, regaining his composure.

He heard a soft grunt of approval from the commandant and the conversation ceased until Brogan drew in by the old cinema. Morley hopped nimbly from the jeep and turned to Brogan. 'Don't stray away, Sergeant,' he said. 'I want you to take Lieutenant Radcliffe and myself to Op-Sud presently.' Morley went directly to Radcliffe who had come to the door. 'Let's go into my office Lieutenant. I want a quick word with you.'

His office was nothing to boast about, just a table, chair, gun rack and a map of Katanga and Kivu provinces which was sellotaped to one wall. The only colour in the room being a Congolese flag that covered the broken window behind the table. Morley eschewed the comfort of the chair for a corner of the table. He scrutinised Radcliffe who stood uneasily to attention in front of him.

'The nominal role,' began Morley. 'You've seen to it I hope.'

'Yes, sir. All six names are on it.'

Morley slapped his thigh, looking pleased. 'Good,' he said. 'Now we'll go to Op-Sud's briefing.'

CHAPTER EIGHT

Operations-South, locally known as Op-Sud, could rightly be called a complex organisation. Operating from the old Bank of Belgium premises it directed the war as best it could in the full knowledge that each and every move on Op-Sud's part held political connotations. The men of 5 Commando, the mercenary navy on Lake Tanganyika, the falsely named Congolese Air Force at Albertville Airport, the Congolese troops stationed in Kivu province and northern Katanga, plus any 6 Commando soldiers in those regions – all under Op-Sud's jurisdiction. The difference between 5 and 6 Commando was solely a matter of nationality. In the main, 6 Commando drew its men from Europe, whereas 5 Commando relied on English speaking nationals reinforced with bilingual Afrikaners and continentals from South Africa.

Although Op-Sud contained regular Belgium Army officers the real power behind it lay in American hands. No aircraft took off without American permission, and no important campaign mounted without the knowledge (and consent) of the youthful looking American military advisers based in Albertville.

Among the Americans were members of the Central Intelligence Agency. They also had a powerful say in military matters, especially with regard to the aircraft flown by the Cuban pilots and the ground crews servicing the planes. Last, and certainly having the least say in the running of Op-Sud, were the officers and men of the Armee Nationale Congolaise.

At 16:30 hours, six days a week, Op-Sud held an operational briefing attended by representatives of all groups. On the day in question Simon Morley, seconded by Lieutenant Radcliffe, drove up to Op-Sud in Sergeant Brogan's jeep to attend the briefing for 5 Commando.

Two Congolese sentries saluted Morley and Radcliffe as they passed through the doors. The two mercenary officers walked around the long counter – a relic from the building's banking days – just inside the doors and then proceeded to the back of the hall which was partitioned off from the front half by a crude screen. Jim Woodall, a young American military adviser, casually dressed in a check shirt and bush trousers, lounged in a chair at a table which was placed near a huge map covering one of the walls in the fabricated room. He nodded to Morley and Radcliffe as they joined him at the table. Three more Americans drifted into the room and sat down at another table on the right of Morley.

A man in a khaki uniform wearing suede shoes on his small feet and a black beret on his head was next to enter the room. His dark bushy eyebrows, meeting over the top of his hawkish nose, exaggerated the depth of his sunken eyes and made his lips appear thinner than they were. He was Machine-g Bradley Chase, commanding officer of the mercenary navy. Three tiny gold stars beneath an insignia of an anchor on his green epaulettes denoted his rank. Chase drew out the chair next to Radcliffe and sat down. Morley leaned forward to talk to him.

'How are things in your section, Brad?' he asked.

'Not enough men. So don't look surprised when I come up to HQ tomorrow morning for a few more recruits.'

Morley made a clucking sound with his tongue and turned to Radcliffe. 'Make a note of that, Lieutenant. Make sure Machine-g Chase is fixed up okay by lunchtime tomorrow.'

'I'll see to it,' promised Radcliffe.

The three young Americans at the table looked across to the entrance of the room. Morley swivelled in his chair and watched Colonel Andre Cartier enter the room with an ANC high-ranking officer. Morley knew Colonel Cartier fairly well. He was a regular Belgian Army officer, but his tall stature, greying hair and his sympathetic features gave him the appearance of an affable schoolmaster. Possibly this was one of the reasons he qualified for his position, since his job required a certain amount of diplomacy. Morley amiably greeted the Colonel, but dismissed the ANC officer with a derisory frown and turned his attention to the large map. As far as Morley was concerned the ANC was the lowest animal that crawled over the earth. He had more respect of the rebels.

Colonel Cartier walked to the front of the tables and stood to the right of the map. He glanced to the door leading into Op-Sud's intelligence office, before facing his audience.

'Good afternoon, gentlemen,' he said in impeccable English, picking up a thin cane from Morley's table. He tapped a small area ringed in red on the map, some twenty miles south-west of the town called Fizi – approximately a day's drive from Baraka in more peaceful times. 'An ANC patrol made contact with a band of rebels, and when I say contact, I mean precisely that.' Colonel Cartier smiled sympathetically at the ANC officer. 'I'm led to believe that both groups surprised each other in the middle of the bush. The ANC patrol commander ordered the rebels to surrender, but they refused and demanded that the ANC should surrender!' He coughed politely behind his hand and smiled at the ANC officer again. 'This pantomime,' went on the Colonel, 'continued for at least ten minutes, with both sides pointing weapons at each other, calling for the other group to surrender. Then the rebels asked the ANC about the health of one of their machine-gs, who had defected to the Government forces a week ago. Do you know what the ANC commander said in reply?'

'What the hell did the guy say?' put in Woodall, hardly believing his ears.

'"He's very well," that is what he said!' 'declared Cartier in an ironical voice. 'And with that, gentlemen, each group backed away and scampered into the bush.'

'Jesus,' remarked one of the other Americans, 'thought for a moment that you were going to tell us that they kissed each other and made up.'

'Believe me, I have related the facts to you precisely as they were given to me. No embroidery whatsoever.' Shaking his head in contempt, the Colonel faced the map once more and pointed his cane to a spot about four miles south of Fizi. 'An ANC patrol hit anti-personnel mines here this morning, losing two men killed and one wounded. No enemy were seen.'

He stopped to light a cigarette and then glanced at Morley. 'We understand that 5 Commando sustained a mortar attack at dawn today, Commandant.'

'Quite correct, Colonel,' answered Morley evenly. 'No damage to speak of and no casualties on our side. Machine-g Heever sent out a patrol, but the rebels beat 'em to the hills.'

'There's always another day,' said Cartier. He looked enquiringly at Machine-g Bradley Chase. 'Have you any news for us Machine-g?'

'I had a P-boat machine-gunning the peninsula this morning after hearing reports of rebel activity on the peninsula tip. The only other news is that I'm commencing a training program for members of the new intake under my command,' tendered Chase in a bored voice.

'And when do you think you'll have them fully trained?' enquired the Colonel. He never had much time for Chase. The man had all the necessary qualities that made up a rogue and scoundrel, but for the sake of harmony Colonel Cartier kept his judgement of Machine-g Bradley Chase to himself. He was quite sure that Chase would make a slip that would expose him for what he was. Conversely, he hoped that Chase's mistake – when it, came – would not make too much of a ripple, thereby rocking the proverbial boat.

Machine-g Chase fingered the lobe of his left ear and frowned mildly at the Colonel's question. 'Depending how soon you want the men for something,' he replied at length.

'As soon as possible. My intelligence officer tells me that gun-running from Tanzania is on the increase. Rebel boats, too, are sneaking across to Kigoma from the peninsula opposite Baraka.'

'I'd better train 'em quick then, hadn't I?' commented Chase.

'I suggest you'd better,' retorted Colonel Cartier. He switched his gaze from Chase to the other men in the room. 'More rebel activity means more work for all of us. My IO has more details about these nightly passages across the lake. He's also collating other information which should be of assistance, so I'll ask him to come out and give you the information we've got to hand.'

He walked across to the intelligence officer's office and opened the door. Inside the room a man was busily preparing a map of Baraka in the surrounding area. He glanced up interestedly as Colonel Cartier shoved his head around the door.

'Would you step outside, Paul?' he was asked. 'I'd like you to brief the men on the gun-running matter. You could also tell them about Lukamba.'

Lagache placed his mapping pen down and picked up a thick notebook. 'Excellent idea, Colonel I'll be with you shortly.'

'Be as quick as you can.' He withdrew to the conference room.

Lagache licked a finger and flipped through the tightly written pages of his notebook. It had been a full two years since he steered his boat into the friendly port of Uvira, arriving more dead than alive from his horrific experience. Even there he could not escape the turmoil of the spreading war. Before he was fully recovered, he found himself in the back of a jeep, heading at breakneck speed along the concrete highway to Bukavu, having the doubtful honour of being among the last persons to leave Uvira before it fell into rebel hands without a shot fired in its defence.

Bukavu didn't capitulate and when Albertville was recaptured in August 1964, he was approached to join the fight against the Simbas. The offer, by Op-Sud, came at the right time. They wanted a man who knew intimately every town and fishing village in their sector of operations. Lagache was an obvious choice to fill the post of intelligence officer. They found him in one of Bukavu's many bars, drinking heavily and nursing a private vendetta against Kimbiti, the rebel who had destroyed his wife, livelihood, and very nearly Lagache himself.

It was not surprising that he accepted Op-Sud's offer. It gave him the positive aim that he so badly needed. It also gave him the opportunity to follow the fortunes of Kimbiti. In all aspects, it was a worthwhile job and would keep him busy until the time came to gather up the tattered traces of his former life.

Lagache discovered the page he wanted. He refreshed his memory from the facts and figures before him and then entered the briefing room where Cartier passed him his cane. Lagache took it and traced an invisible line on the large operations map from the Tanzanian port of Kigoma, across the lake, to the peninsula near Baraka.

'The rebels,' began Lagache, 'are ferrying ammunition, mines, guns and other war supplies to this part of the peninsula by night. The supplies are then taken along footpaths into the mountains just south of Baraka. There, they are distributed proportionally to rebel groups operating around Baraka. Some of these supplies are also going to rebels in the Fizi area.

'The enemy isn't stupid. The rebels use other routes to make sure the supplies get through in ever-increasing amounts.' Lagache tapped the tip of the cane on a small lakeside village which had been underlined in red on the map. 'This fishing village is called Lueba. It's roughly twelve miles north of Baraka and is being used occasionally for the landing of supplies from Tanzania.'

He paused briefly to allow his words to sink home. 'Now, here comes the rub. Both routes are virtually nothing when compared with the quantity of rebel supplies being brought into Lukamba from Tanzania and Rwanda.'

'And Lukamba is the largest rebel town up there since we captured Baraka,' prompted Morley.

'Correct,' said Lagache. He gazed at Morley. 'I understand that 5 Commando may be called upon to take Lukamba in the near future. You should, therefore, be interested in the latest, developments in that part of the world.' He saw Morley's cold eyes widen fractionally. Radcliffe dug into his short pockets and extracted a small pad and ballpoint pen. 'We all know,' went on Lagache, 'that Lukamba is the rebel HQ. We also know that there is a big arms depot in or near the town. But what we didn't know – until late yesterday, in fact – was that gold is being ferried through Lukamba to pay for supplies coming from Rwanda. Tanzania is a different proposition. The rebels get everything free from that country. Another point which should interest you, although we haven't positive proof, is the rumour that Chinese military advisers are operating in the vicinity of Lukamba.'

'Yes, very interesting,' murmured Morley, half watching Radcliffe scribbling down the information.

'Lately, the rebel strength has increased from six hundred to eight hundred men in Lukamba. Louis Kimbiti, promoted to colonel not long ago, is now a general and in sole command – if that's the word – of Lukamba and the surrounding areas right down to Baraka.'

'What's our Air Force doing in Lukamba?' put in Chase.

'Attacking it from the air,' said Woodall. 'We can't do it every day as we haven't the planes. We've got to carry out sorties over Baraka and Fizi, besides the other places,' he added pointedly.

Chase grunted an acknowledgement It was a good answer, and he wasn't in a position to fault it. He lit a cigarette and sat back, staring at the operations map in front of him.

'Are Kimbiti and his staff still holed up on your plantation just outside Lukamba?' cut in Morley to Lagache.

'As far as I know,' He glanced at Cartier. 'I've covered the new developments at Lukamba. Is there anything else you'd like me to say on the other districts?'

'I don't think so, Paul.' The Colonel looked around the room. 'Any questions?'

'Only one,' said Morley. 'Where's all this gold coming from?'

Lagache pointed his cane to a mountainous area on the map, less than twenty miles due west of Lukamba.

'Here,' he said to Morley. 'It's a gold mine which we thought was worked out. It seems the rebels have found a vein which had been overlooked. This can be the only logical explanation, because prisoners tell me that gold is being taken through Lukamba from this district. I must be honest with you and say that it is a calculated assumption on my part that they've reopened the workings. Naturally, if I hear of anything to the contrary, I shall notify you, Commandant.' added Lagache.

'Please do,' said Morley.

Lagache gave the cane back to Cartier and returned to his office. He closed the door and helped himself to a cigarette from a pack in the top drawer of his desk. Sinking into the desk chair he lit the cigarette with a Zippo lighter, a birthday present from Jim Woodall. His hand was shaking as he pocketed the lighter.

Lagache knew why. Sometime soon 5 Commando would try to clear the road from Baraka to Uvira. If their past record was any guide, it was quite likely that they would succeed. He could then go home. But would he want to when the time came?

Nostalgic memories flooded over him in traumatic waves. What would it be like without Marie? It was a question continually haunting him. And there was only one way of answering it.

'Merde!' he hissed in a fit of depression. He tossed his notebook into a wire tray and began working feverishly, trying to blot out the awful nightmare of Marie's death.

CHAPTER NINE

In the dark, dank front room of the first bungalow past the 5 Commando cookhouse, Toby Ashton raised a sleepy hand to fend off a particularly vicious mosquito. It had been a ceaseless battle as he tried to rid himself of the persistent hordes of mosquitos at large in the room. And he had lost every round. The mosquito attacked again, buzzing towards his face at a higher intensity.

Ashton slapped at it wildly, jack-knifing his body into a sitting position on his stretcher. Then he saw why the mosquitos had pestered him all night. His mosquito net had collapsed. He glared balefully around the darkened room, the net draped willy-nilly over his hunched form.

When his eyes became accustomed to the dark he noticed with sadistic satisfaction that his mosquito net was not the only one which had collapsed. Bream's net had also fallen down, fully exposing his bare feet to any hungry mosquito that cared to land.

The seven other persons in the room apparently had no trouble with their nets and were sleeping the sleep of angels. Ashton looked out of the window and was mildly surprised to see the dawn was approaching. He yawned tiredly, wishing all manner of curses on the Congo's insect life.

Now that sleep had evaded him, he decided to cut his losses and get up. On exploring the bungalow the previous evening he discovered that there was only a very small bathroom. Now he could be the first one in it. Having made this momentous decision, he threw off the useless mosquito net and put his feet on the concrete floor. He slipped on a pair of khaki drills and his newly issued grey socks but had difficulty for a minute in lacing up his combat boots. His comrades had begun to waken by the time he was ready to make for the bathroom.

Ashton closed the bathroom door and fumbled for the light switch. Suddenly he remembered the bungalow lacked electricity. The fact also reminded him from yesterday's experiences that the bungalow lacked running water too.

Totally frustrated, he decided to try the cookhouse next door for some hot water. He walked into the backyard of the cookhouse with washing kit and towel tucked under his arm. His initiative was rewarded by the sight of three gigantic cooking pots steaming away on makeshift ranges. He spied a bucket, picked it up and headed for the cooking pots.

A Congolese civilian trotted into the yard as Ashton dipped the bucket into the first pot. The man clucked in disapproval as he watched Ashton carry the bucket of hot water over to the corner of the yard, thoroughly pleased with himself.

His roommates were awkwardly washing and shaving from mugs of cold water when he returned. He gazed at them in superior fashion and repacked his washing kit. Shortly afterwards the call went out that breakfast was ready. Ashton grabbed his mess tin and eating utensils, but Bream and Morgan beat him out of the front door.

He looked up at the sky as he walked with them to the cookhouse. The sky was devoid of clouds and the early morning sun slanted deep shadows from the leafy trees across their path. The leaves hung heavy on the branches, undisturbed by even a trace of wind. The three men could already feel the the sun's heat on their faces as they walked along the road. All the climatic signs pointed to a typical Congolese day. Hot and humid.

Sergeant Brogan put in an appearance at the cookhouse. After pinning a large note on the door that the intake were to parade at 07:30 hours, he went inside a room exclusively reserved for Base HQ personnel to await breakfast.

At 07:30 hours sharp, after a breakfast of watery porridge, the mercenaries lined up in three ranks outside Base HQ. Radcliffe arrived by truck from the Hotel du Lac at 07:35 and Brogan brought the mercenaries to attention. After returning Brogan's crisp salute, Radcliffe informed him that he wanted six volunteers to join the navy.

When Brogan found the six volunteers, he was to pick a further forty men, distribute arms and ammunition among them, and make sure that they were packed and ready to leave on the *Rachelle* by 13:00 hours that day for Baraka.

'I'll have forty bodies ready for embarkation by midday, and six volunteers for the navy within the hour.' declared Brogan.

'Very good, Sergeant,' said Radcliffe. 'I want the six for the navy in my office as soon as possible.'

'You'll have 'em sir,' he replied with conviction.

Brogan saluted Radcliffe again before turning to the intake.

'Every man jack who has done service in any navy, take one step forward!' Ten men stepped forward. Among them was Ashton. Brogan scrutinised each one in turn, then he crooked a finger and beckoned Ashton. 'For the record, you've just volunteered for the Congo Navy,' said Brogan in a derogatory tone of voice. 'Now double into Lieutenant Radcliffe's office.' He picked out five more recruits and sent them scurrying after Ashton.

The remaining four were told to fall back into line. When his order had been obeyed, Brogan struck a dramatic pose and said, 'All previous contract men will now fall out and form three ranks on my right.' He waited impatiently for the mercenaries to sort themselves out before counting them. Twenty-three. He needed another seventeen.

He looked at the depleted ranks on his left. 'How many of you guys can handle an FN rifle?'

A mass of arms went up, including Bream's. Brogan counted off seventeen, Bream among them, and ordered them to join the veterans. He then spoke to a mercenary who wore the silver star of sergeant on his green epaulettes.

'Take this squad over, Sergeant, and march 'em into the armoury. Issue each man with an FN and two hundred rounds of ammo. When you've done that, march 'em back to their billets to pack their kit. I want them back here by 12:00 hours on the dot, ready to truck down to the docks. They're embarking on the *Rachelle* at 13:00 hours.'

The Sergeant, a stocky man in his thirties, placed them into one line to file into Base HQ and through to the armoury. They reappeared with automatic rifles and ammunition. Meanwhile, Brogan dismissed the other mercenaries. They drifted back to the bungalows with Brogan's words ringing in their ears about staying on base and reporting back to HQ after lunch.

Bream and Morgan also made their way back to their bungalow, carrying their rifles and bandoliers of 762mm bullets. Bream had immense difficulty in suppressing his excitement. One day he was in Johannesburg, the next day in Albertville, and soon he would be sailing up Lake Tanganyika bound for Baraka. In nervous anticipation, he drummed his fingers on the butt of his rifle as he entered the bungalow.

In Radcliffe's office, Toby Ashton and the other five men destined for the navy were ordered to get their kit together. When they had done that, they were to place it on the truck which Radcliffe had parked outside the building and climb aboard themselves. The truck would depart for Albertville at 09:00 hours.

Dryden, the recruit who had fallen foul of Sergeant Brogan on the first day, was one of the men told to stay on base. He wiped his hot brow as he trudged back to his billet, thinking longingly of the ice-cold beer that could be his if he were allowed into town.

He badly needed a drink. Several drinks for that matter. In Johannesburg he was never without some form of alcohol, and yesterday's forced abstinence had heightened his desire for liquor to a screaming intensity. Radcliffe's promise of being allowed off base that night had faded to a bunch of meaningless words. Brogan's distinct order about staying on base had also become transparent. His body, used to large quantities of drink, was steadily taking command of his senses. Dryden clenched his fists, hoping to beat off the feeling. It was no use. He shook his head in despair, realising that he could neither fight nor dismiss his need for alcohol. Now, it was just a question of slipping into town unseen.

His chance arrived on seeing another recruit by the name of Theron who, at that very moment, had dived into an overgrown garden of a house bordering the other road into town. Dryden knew Theron from the Savoy bar in Johannesburg. He was also aware that Theron was as much an alcoholic as himself. Moreover, it did not require a crystal ball to guess where Theron was going and Dryden intended joining him. He checked quickly to ensure that nobody was watching him before sprinting into the undergrowth, hoping to catch up with Theron.

Ashton tossed his kitbag over the tailboard of the truck and climbed up after it. He was the last recruit to arrive, and a host of willing hands helped him aboard. He gasped his gratitude and sank thankfully on to his kitbag. He had never moved so fast for many a year as he had in the last hour, since Brogan picked him for the navy. It was not even 09:00 hours, yet his khaki shirt was wet with perspiration. Ashton felt a twinge of doubt about his hasty decision to join 5 Commando.

Too late to do anything about it now, he thought, squinting up at the deep, almost overpowering sky. He pulled his beret down to shade his eyes from the sun's glare and made up his mind to make the best of it. After all, he surmised, there wasn't much chance of being extradited from the Congo.

A member of the base staff stepped into the cab and the truck moved off for the docks. They had a flurried view of Albertville as they drove through the town and into a square overlooked by a shell-scarred church. The truck halted by the Albertville railway station on the left side of the square.

Their driver told them to jump down with their kit and go through the main entrance. They carried out his instructions only to find themselves looking at two hundred yards of railway line, curving towards a wooden catwalk. Beyond the catwalk were the squat concrete dock buildings, partly submerged in water. 'What now?' enquired Ashton, turning on the driver.

'You see that white ship over there?' The ship, half-hidden by the dock buildings, appeared to Ashton as some type of large pleasure steamer, a legacy of more peaceful days. 'She's the *Albertville* where Machine-g Chase has his headquarters. He's in command of the navy and you lot are to report to him.'

'But that ship seems miles away!' exclaimed a recruit, fumbling with his kitbag and suitcase. 'How the heck do we get to her?'

'By walking along the railway line and on to the catwalk, but watch your step. That catwalk is a bit rickety. It was built in a hurry after the lake level rose.' He handed a sealed envelope to Ashton. 'Give this to Machine-g Chase when you report to him.' Smiling sympathetically the mercenary added, 'You blokes are on your own now. I'm returning to HQ. Good luck and have fun on the water.' He left them staring at the distant ship.

'The sooner we get going, the sooner we'll get there,' muttered Ashton to the others.

They humped their kitbags on to their shoulders, picked up the rest of their belongings, and began plodding along the track. All six of them saw what the HQ driver meant when they started staggering along the catwalk. It was extremely unsafe and the odd missing board heightened their chances of falling into the murky waters below. Somehow, they completed the journey without mishap and walked up the *Albertville* gangplank. A mercenary officer was waiting for them at the top.

'Just in time,' he said, glancing at his watch. 'Machine-g Chase is expecting you right away, but first I'll take you to your quarters.'

With the officer leading, they went below where he showed them their bunks. They dumped their kit and followed him back on deck again. He took them up a polished wooden ladder, through the bridge, to Chase's cabin. The door whipped open on the second knock, leaving them huddled under the abrupt scrutiny of Chase.

'So, you six are the replacements,' he said stonily.

'Yes sir,' said Ashton, wondering whether he should have I said 'Aye, aye, sir.' His reply, however, passed without comment as Chase stretched out his hand and took the sealed envelope from Ashton.

Chase ripped it open and pulled out a letter. Ashton noticed a list of names and assumed that the names referred to them. His assumption was correct. Chase tossed the letter on to a desk in his cabin.

'Right,' he began in a clipped tone. 'You men will be training on our P-boats and Swifts. After which you'll be assigned for operational duties on the lake. A couple of you might even go on Big Daddy, but first we'll see how you progress. Reveille is at 05:30 hours, compulsory swimming at 06:00 hours, followed by breakfast at 06:45 hours. Training commences at 07:30 hours each morning until further notice. Lieutenant Olivier here, will give you any additional information you require.' Chase shot a look at Olivier, the mercenary officer. 'Take them away now and start training them as soon as possible.'

With that, Chase shut his cabin door.

'I suggest you unpack your kit first of all and then meet me up on deck in fifteen minutes time,' said Olivier, escorting them off the bridge.

They soon had their kit unpacked and went on deck. They found Olivier on the port side, leaning over the ship's rails.

He threw away the cigarette he was smoking and called them over. 'There's one of the P-boats,' he said, pointing over the rails at an open grey motorboat with a menacing .50 calibre machine-gun mounted in the bows. Two mercenaries were in the boat, fiddling around with the powerful engine. 'The P-boat usually has a crew of two, but sometimes we have three aboard. "Olivier then directed their attention to a long, sleek grey craft which was anchored some way off. The boat reminded Ashton of the wartime air-sea rescue crafts. 'That's a Swift,' he announced. 'We've got three altogether, but the other two are out on the lake.'

'What's this Big Daddy which Machine-g Chase mentioned?' asked a recruit standing next to Ashton, and whose name he thought was Bashford.

Olivier smiled. 'You mean *Le Ermens*, but her code name is Big Daddy. She's a converted trawler, bristling with .50 Brownings and 75mm recoilless rifles. The rebs hate her. She's due in port tomorrow and then you'll see her for yourselves.'

'On which class of boat do we begin our training?' enquired Ashton.

'The P-boats,' said Olivier. He attracted the attention of one of the mercenaries in the P-boat below. 'Bring your craft, alongside the dock, Evans,' he called.

Evans waved an acknowledgement and replaced the engine cover. He fired the motors and, with his mate at the wheel, steered aft of the *Albertville* and neatly manoeuvred the P-boat against the dock.

Olivier turned to his group. 'You'll spend the rest of this morning learning about the P-boat's engine. After lunch I'll get Evans to take you out in the bay, three at a time, where you can try your hands piloting the boat. Remind me at lunch to find you all some black berets. We don't wear the green beret in the navy.' Olivier straightened his back and moved away from the ship's rails. Just as he did, an empty Vat 69 bottle sailed over his head and splashed into the lake. Ashton glanced up in surprise and caught a glimpse of Machine-g Chase on the upper deck. The next moment he heard Chase slamming his cabin door. Ashton looked questioningly at Olivier. The Lieutenant gave a rueful grin.

'The Machine-g likes his drink, but take a tip from me,' he said. 'Keep a wide berth of him when he's had a few pots too many, sometimes he thinks he's the fastest gun in the west.'

'I'll believe it,' said Ashton

'You'd better. Now let's get down to the P-boat.'

For the first time that day Brogan was in fair humour, having rounded up the first shipment of men for Baraka and organised the naval replacements in record time. He lingered on the long veranda at Base HQ, idly gazing at the row of banana trees growing near the grass verge. The rest of the morning was his to use as he thought fit. Taking a last look at the banana trees, Brogan decided to get his head down for a while. He was about to go inside when he noticed an African cycling up the road, waving to him.

'What the hell's up now?' grunted Brogan, watching the man dismount and run up to him.

He soon found out, much to his chagrin. And the more the African gibbered away in French, the more Brogan's pleasant frame of mind receded. He was positively ill tempered by the time the African had finished speaking.

'So, they won't, won't they?' he expostulated, more to himself than to the African. 'We'll soon see about that!' He hitched up his webbing belt, brushed the African aside and strode grimly to his jeep. Brogan took the first corner like a madman and roared towards the main street. The jeep slewed right as he drove on to the street, the engine whining crazily. Brogan wrestled with the wheel, simultaneously slamming the gear in with a resounding thump. He increased speed until he was almost level with a narrow dirt road intersecting the main street on the right. Again, the engine whined when Brogan braked, changed down to a lower gear, and sent the jeep shooting up the narrow dirt road. Sixty yards on he pulled in sharply beside a shabby shebeen. The place vibrated with the sound of colourful Congolese music, but Brogan wasn't interested in the music. He had come for something else.

Brogan jumped from the jeep and punched open the shebeen's doors. The bar and dancefloor were crowded to capacity. Brogan began shoving his way towards the front. Above the musical din and shouting voices, he heard the black proprietor call his name and point to the far corner. Brogan grunted and recommenced elbowing another passage through the swaying, sweating, shining bodies until he neared a table hidden by a group of screaming Congolese. They saw him and fell back to let him reach the table. Brogan scowled as his thick hands gripped the backs of two chairs.

'So, you won't pay for your drinks, eh?' he yelled, his face dark with anger, his eyes glinting furiously.

The two mercenaries, Dryden and Theron, turned as one in their chairs. They were drunk and their eyes weren't focusing properly, but they knew who was standing behind them by Brogan's Canadian accent, which had cut through the smoke, din and chatter like a swish of Toledo steel. He hoisted them to their feet by their shirt collars. 'Well, that's damned tough on Casper,' hissed Brogan. 'He knows you shouldn't be in here. And by Jesus, so do you! What's more, both of you are gonna pay for your drinks in a way you won't like!' he bellowed, glaring at each man in turn. His eyes closed to mere slits on recognising Dryden. 'Unless my memory's playing me tricks, I think you and I had a little talk yesterday. Dryden ain't it?'

Tiny beads of sweat glistened on Dryden's forehead. He gulped, licked his lips nervously and gave a drunken nod.

'Oh, Dryden,' said Brogan heavily. 'You're really gonna pay for flouting orders.'

He got a firmer grip on the back of their shirt collars and hustled them through the throng of Africans. Brogan gave them both a vicious shove through the doorway. They lost their precarious balance and fell headlong on to the dirt road. Brogan walked around them, kicking them to their feet. 'Get up! Get up, you drunken bastards. Get up into the back of my jeep. If you want to see tomorrow, you'd better hang on really good, because I don't intend stopping if you fall over the side. I'll just reverse over you bums. And I ain't joking!'

On the way back to 5 Commando Headquarters, Brogan deliberately drove over the worst patches he could find in the road. He swung the jeep hard around the last corner and had the sadistic satisfaction of hearing them slide helplessly across the jeep's metal floor. As a finale, Brogan brought the jeep to a bone-jarring halt and was rewarded by a heavy thud in the back of his seat as one of them piled up against it. Brogan got out of the jeep and watched Dryden and Theron climb stiffly into a sitting position.

'Don't think that you bastards are gonna stay there and pass the time of day,' he said in a menacing voice. 'The fun's only beginning. Now get off my jeep and stand to attention in the middle of the road. Move, you bastards. Move!'

In a drunken daze they started descending from the jeep, but their progress was not fast enough for Brogan. His powerful arms flashed to grab their belts. Then, with a mighty jerk, he pitched them off the vehicle and into the road.

'So, you guys are keen to roll about in the dirt,' he growled. 'With luck you'll be rolling in the dirt some more. Now get to your miserable feet and stand to attention.'

Dryden and Theron, their limbs twitching with anxiety, tried their best to stand upright. Brogan saw that they were still very much under the influence of alcohol. He took stock of the pathetic situation, watching them squint into the bright rays of the sun. Brogan glowered. 'The sun's damned hot, but you drinkies are gonna be hotter. I promise you that, even I don't promise you anything else.' He pointed his baton towards the cookhouse, fifty yards up the road. 'When I give you the order you will double to the gateway of the cookhouse, about turn and double past me to the bend in this road. You will about turn at the bend and double past me again to the cookhouse gates. You will keep this up until I tell you otherwise, Do I make myself clear?' he bellowed angrily.

'Yes, Sergeant,' they blurted back in unison.

Brogan stepped back three paces, swung his baton beneath his right armpit and ordered them to turn left. Dryden and Theron obeyed like badly manipulated puppets. 'Right turn!' yelled Brogan, purple-faced. 'We'll have that drill movement done again – and done properly! Left turn!' Brogan was still not satisfied. 'Right turn, you stupid bastards! Left turn! Right turn! Left turn! Double march!' They doubled down the road. Brogan waited until they were level with the cookhouse. 'Abaht turn!' he yelled in a stentorian voice. 'Hup, one-two, hup, one-two. For Christ's sake! Stop mincing along like bloody fairies. Get your feet up!'

Their knees were well up by their stomachs when they doubled past Brogan.

'Keep going until I order you to stop.'

Brogan retired under the long veranda, watching their punishing progress from the shade. Both recruits showed signs of flagging after fifteen minutes, but Brogan refused them mercy. 'You're dawdling again!' he shouted. 'Get those feet up!'

Another fifteen minutes ticked by and the tropical sun began to take its toll with a vengeance. Theron's legs gave way, and he folded up in the road. Dryden vaguely heard his mate collapse, and he immediately slowed his pace. 'Keep going, Dryden. Nobody told you to slow down,' rapped Brogan. He called for someone inside Base HQ to fetch a bucket. The bucket duly arrived. Brogan grabbed it and stalked to a tap by the right-hand corner of the building. He filled the bucket with cold water and walked across to the panting figure of Theron.

'Theron!' he barked.

Theron gazed up feebly and was compensated with the full force of the water thrown into his face. 'On your feet, Theron. I want to see you doubling again.' He struggled gamely to his feet and staggered away with Brogan's commands ringing in his ears.

Old Wrecked convoy from ambush

B26 flying low giving air support

Local girl gathering water

B26 Aircraft lined up on Albertville Airfield

B26 close up

Albertville from the air

Mercenary transport from airport

Albertville graveyard

Mercenary graves

Palm tree lined street

Albertville Main Street

5 Commando HQ

Abandoned European house

Outside 5 Commando HQ

P-boat

Le Ermens (Big Daddy)

Helicopter flying overhead

Peninsula and sunken ship

Peninsula beach

B26 flying across the Peninsula coastline

T28 aircraft

Hole in the wall club

Patrolling on road

Exposed anti-personnel mine

Helicopter flying wounded

On guard duty

Mercenaries' funeral

Gun salute for funeral

5 Commando radio room

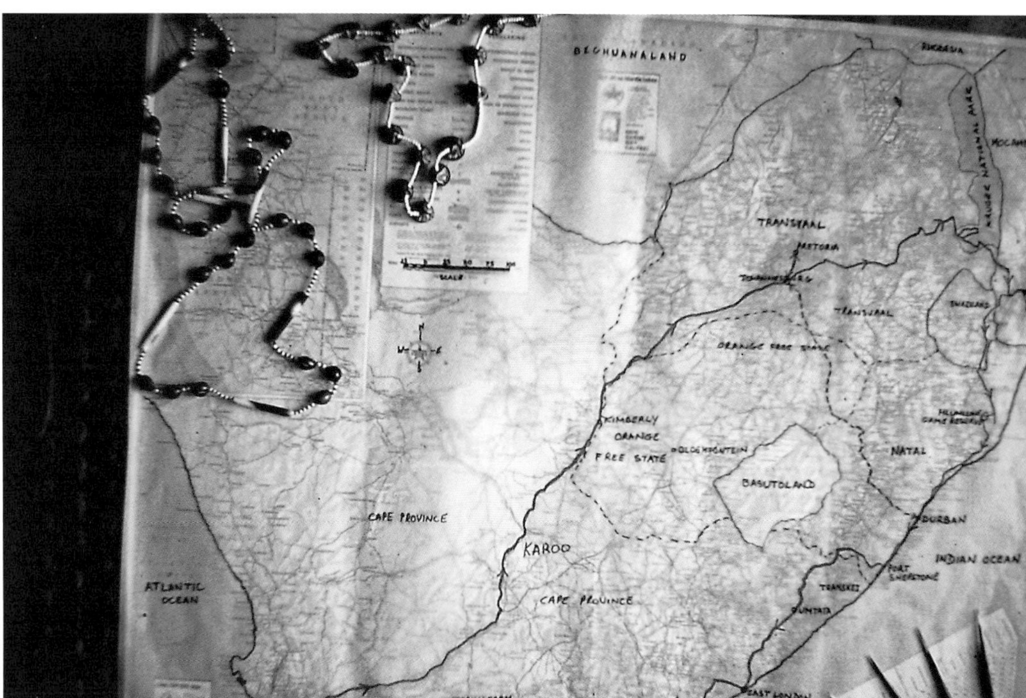

Mission map of Congo

Patrolling through elephant grass

Spotted while patrolling, attacking now

Above left: 76mm gun with operator and chain feeder

Above right: 76mm gun

Left: Burning rebel villages to the ground

ANC with coffins

Ferret car

Broken bridge

Repairing and testing bridge

Guard duty with 5ks Chinese carbine

View of Nungula village

Road patrol

Push to Lukamba

Push to Lukamba

Relief of Simba stronghold

6 Commando hospital

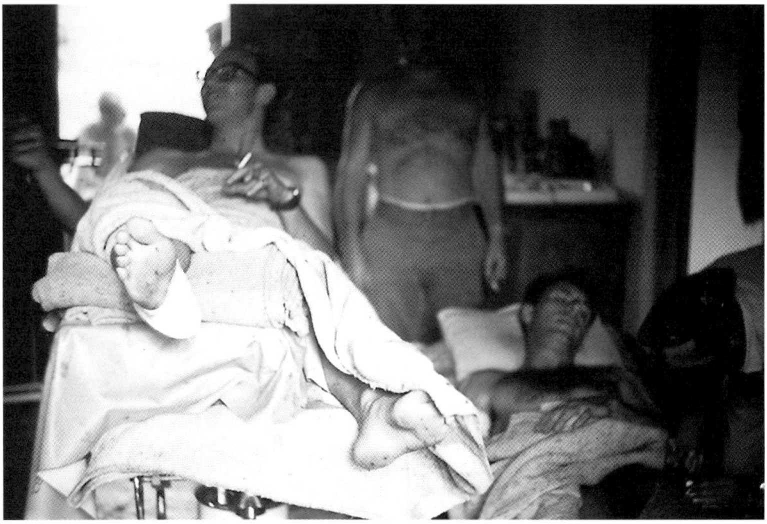

6 Commando hospital ward

Mercenary with Afrikaans

Waiting at Elizabethville Airport

T-28 flying over Albertville

Chilling by the River

Ruandi Cattle

L-R Force tiger pin, 5 Commando patch, Silver Seargent stars on mercenary lapels

5 Commando's own OK corral

M'Boko

Air Congo DC-06 Kamina airport

Hippo in Lake Tanganyika

Above: G.P.M.G Post

Left: Elder with a Pipe

Below: DC-06 arriving 2 hours late at Elizabethville

Above: Captured rebels

Below left: Relaxing on the river

Below right: Dried aiver

Mercenaries with guides, Baraka

Baraka regatta

Baraka regatta

Baraka regatta

Albertville
from water

Air drop

30th June
Congo got
independence
and celebrated

Parade for
Congo gaining
independence

30th June
parade

'That's his object is it?' mumbled Dryden, perspiration streaming down his heaving chest. 'Well, we'll see.'

Muttering mechanically, Dryden doubled to the corner for what seemed to be the millionth time. As he turned, he saw Theron collapse again, retching violently. Brogan walked towards him with another pail of water. Theron threw up on the road, before Brogan could fling the water over him. Without a glimmer of pity Brogan emptied the bucket over his shaking body and ordered him to stand up. Theron simply vomited again, inadvertently on Brogan's gleaming boots.

'You fucking filthy animal!' he screeched, kicking the luckless recruit in the ribs. 'It'll make you lick 'em clean. Do you hear? I'll make you lick 'em clean!'

But Theron was past caring. He had fainted. With scanty ceremony Brogan dragged him to the roadside, then directed his full attention on Dryden. Rivulets of sweat rolled down Dryden's forehead, stinging his eyes. Although he could scarcely see, he could not help but notice the thick form of Brogan standing a yard away, surveying him with open hate.

'You – won't – break – me,' panted Dryden, his breath coming in painful gasps.

Brogan maintained his scrutiny until it dawned on him that other people were watching too. Two of the admin staff had come out and, judging from their expressions, their sympathies plainly lay with Dryden. Brogan gritted his teeth in vexation and looked at Dryden once more. Dryden kept going, stubbornly refusing to let Brogan have the satisfaction of seeing him drop.

'Trying to make a clown out of me, eh?' mouthed Brogan sullenly. 'I'll soon fix you, my lad.'

He strode into Base HQ and reappeared with an FN rifle minus its magazine. He walked into the middle of the road, waited for Dryden to come within reach, and threw the rifle at him. Instinct made him catch it. He staggered back a yard, clutching the FN to his chest.

'Get that rifle above your head and keep it there!' Dryden halted in sheer disbelief and gaped at Brogan. 'Who told you to stop? Keep doubling. Let's see if you're the hard case you think you are.'

He raised the FN above his head, his shoulder shaking with exertion. The limit of endurance was approaching fast, but Dryden somehow managed to put one foot in front of the other. He mumbled inanely as he zigzagged up the road, the cruel weight of the rifle bearing down on his aching shoulders. Radcliffe, attracted by Brogan's shouting, came to join the onlookers on the veranda. He noted with concern the twitching person of Theron by the grass verge before his eyes focused on the staggering figure of Dryden, head painfully bowed as he tried to double with the FN rifle above him.

'Brogan's crucifying him,' Radcliffe overheard someone say. Radcliffe, from what he could see, thought so too. He hurried to Brogan's side.

'Disobedience, sir,' flashed Brogan before Radcliffe could ask. 'Drunk on duty and disobeying orders to stay on base.'

'How long have you been drilling them?'

'Not long enough, sir,' he said crisply. 'It's the drink that's doing 'em.'

'I sincerely hope it is, Sergeant. I don't want them dying on us.'

'Nobody's gonna die, sir.'

'You're the best judge of that, Sergeant.'

'Yes, sir. I'm the best judge of that,' he replied, containing his anger with difficulty.

Frowning uneasily, Radcliffe turned his back on the disquieting scene and retraced his steps to his office. Highly disgruntled by Radcliffe's remarks, Brogan vented his anger on Dryden. 'Straighten those arms, Dryden. I want to see that rifle way up.'

It annoyed him intensely that behind him the HQ staff were willing Dryden to martyrdom. Suddenly he noticed that mercenaries from the bungalows were also watching the battle of wills between Dryden and himself. Two audiences proved too much for Brogan's frail patience. He stormed into the road as Dryden tottered by.

'Straighten your arms, blast you! And get your stomach in. You're not pregnant!'

Brogan's incessant bellowing beat a hollow cacophony in Dryden's thumping head. Wheezing like an old man, he plodded on defiantly, the road wavering violently in front of his eyes. His determination succeeded too well. Brogan let out a yell of desperation and lunged at Dryden's back with his fist. Dryden screamed in pain. The rifle flew from his grasp, and he cartwheeled to the ground, his hands clawing the air.

'Got you, you bastard,' gloated Brogan triumphantly. 'Got you, you bastard,' he repeated in a lower note, realising that his victory wasn't such a victory after all.

He picked up the FN and hauled Dryden on to the grass. Even his limited knowledge told him that Dryden would take some time in recovering from such drastic punishment. Brogan refilled the bucket and poured water on to the fatigued recruit's upturned features. He tossed away the bucket just as Commandant Morley sped around the corner in a jeep, driven by one of the American military advisers. Morley alighted from the jeep, thanking the young American for the lift. The American grinned appreciatively and drove off. Brogan sprang to attention and saluted Morley. The Commandant gestured at Dryden and Theron. 'What happened to them?'

'They flouted routine orders, sir. So, I gave 'em a spot of drill. Drunk as skunks they was, sir.'

Morley's face hardened. 'Toss them into the Box for the night and repatriate them in the morning. But before you take them to the prison, I want to discuss an important, matter with you and Lieutenant Radcliffe.'

'Has something cropped up from Op-Sud?' enquired Radcliffe as they entered the radio room.

'Yes, plenty,' said Morley going over to the radio operator. 'Baraka may be coming under attack within the next thirty-six hours. A rebel column is heading that way from Kafulo right now. One of the T-28 pilots saw the column when he was flying back to base, but he couldn't do anything about it as he had used up all ammunition.'

'Just our luck,' sniffed Radcliffe.

'Luck or not, Machine-g Heever at Baraka has to be warned about this development. We can also inform him that troops are on their way to help him out,' returned Morley. 'Trust the rebels to think of attacking now when the Baraka garrison is so below strength.' He glanced at Radcliffe and Brogan.

'I presume you've got the forty men for embarkation on the *Rachelle*.'

'They're parading at 12:00 hours, sir,' announced Brogan.

'It's a damned good thing the *Rachelle* is sailing today,' said Radcliffe. 'At least we were caught pulling our trousers up.'

His quip failed to amuse Morley.

'Let's not get carried away, Lieutenant,' replied Morley in a cold voice. 'The rebels can still beat our men to Baraka.' He picked up a signal pad from the radio operator's table and quickly wrote a message. 'Raise Baraka and send this,' he instructed the radio operator. He then turned to Radcliffe. 'Find yourself a vehicle and get down to Machine-g

Chase. Tell him to round up every available Swift and P-boat, especially the ones on patrol, and get them to Baraka. You can tell him to leave one to escort the *Rachelle*. I'm going to Baraka myself, but by helicopter. That's all, Lieutenant.'

Radcliffe rushed from the room.

'Do you still want me, sir?' put in Brogan, trying to be helpful.

'No. Carry on with your normal duties, Sergeant, but just make sure those forty men are well and truly ensconced on the *Rachelle* and ready for action,' said Morley, dismissing him. When Brogan had gone, he leaned against the table listening to the radio operator trying to make contact with Barka.

'Queen, Queen, Queen,' repeated the operator into his microphone. 'This is Paradise calling, this is Paradise calling. Are you receiving me? Over.'

He flicked a switch and listened intently. He breathed with relief as the radio operator on duty in Baraka came on the air.

'Paradise this is Queen, I am receiving you five-by-five. Send your message. Over.'

'Rebel column coming your position. I say rebel column coming your position from Kafulo direction. I say Kafulo direction. Column estimated thirty-six hours from your position. Reinforcements leaving Paradise at 13:00 hours on *Rachelle*. ETA 17:00 hours tomorrow. Sunray arriving at your position at 16:00 hours today. End of message.'

'Paradise from Queen. Message received. Roger and out.'

The operator pushed the microphone away from him and reached up to switch off the set. Morley stopped him. 'Keep tuned into Queen and let me know immediately if Machine-g Heever comes on the air.' You'll find me in my office for the next hour.'

Brogan in the meantime had taken Dryden and Theron to the Congolese prison and was on his way back to HQ. It was 11:50 hours, and he fervently hoped the men for Baraka had started parading. It wouldn't do for something to go wrong with Commandant Morley prowling around the base. Three military trucks drove away from outside Op-Sud, heading towards 5 Commando Headquarters. Brogan saw them in his wing mirror and the tension inside him diminished slightly. At least the transportation for the mercenaries would be on time.

Radcliffe arrived back a few minutes before Brogan. He was pleased to see that a number of men were parading with their kit and rifles. He went inside Base HQ and was promptly called into Morley's office.

'We're thin on non-com's for this batch,' Morley informed him, jabbing a finger at the nominal role on his desk, 'we want three more sergeants.'

They scanned the role together.

'How about Inglesole?' suggested Radcliffe. 'He's an ex-contract man and doesn't panic easily.'

'Okay, we'll have him,' said Morley, producing a pen. He placed a tick next to Inglesole's name.

'This chap Marvin was an NCO in the British Army, according to his papers,' pointed out Radcliffe.

'He'll do and now we need one more. Ah!' Morley pointed his pen to Morgan's name. 'We'll have him too.' Brogan's raucous voice filtered through the office walls as he ordered the men outside to stand at ease. Morley looked at Radcliffe.

'These three bodies should be on parade now. Go and fetch them.'

Radcliffe escorted Inglesole, Marvin and Morgan into Morley's office. Morley opened a drawer, pushed some papers aside and took out three sets of tiny stars. 'I'm promoting you three to the rank of sergeant, he said handing out the stars. Now join the parade again.'

They stepped back, saluted smartly, and departed from Morley's office.

'Come on you three,' Brogan shouted as they came out of the main door. 'I ain't gonna wait all day for you.'

'Screw yourself,' retorted Morgan with heavy emphasis, pointing at the set of stars in his hand.

Brogan's thick lips curled back in surprise and disgust. He spat into the dust as they collected their gear. The trucks backed up and they climbed on board with the other mercenaries. Bream shifted his kit, to give Morgan room beside him.

'Congratulations on being made sergeant,' he said.

'Thanks, but it doesn't mean much. Anyhow I can do with the extra pay,' answered Morgan with a grin.

The trio of trucks moved off for the docks, leaving Brogan alone in front of Base HQ. He spat again before walking inside.

Word of the imminent embarkation had obviously got around. Awaiting at the railway station was a gang of Congolese all eager to help the mercenaries with their kit. With their assistance the awkward journey to the docks was negotiated without injury.

The mercenaries paid them off and then strolled to the dockside. There, with streaks of rust showing redly through the black painted hull, was the *Rachelle*. They gazed at the narrow square-bottomed boat with jaundiced eyes.

'Good grief!' uttered Marvin with amazement. 'Are we going on that?'

'We'll be packed like sardines,' said Bream to Morgan.

'Surely there's been a mistake.'

Morgan gave a cynical laugh. 'It's no mistake. That's the *Rachelle*.'

A young Second Lieutenant from 5 Commando joined them on the quay. 'I'm Lieutenant Ford,' he announced, 'and you're in my charge until we reach Baraka. Now before we get aboard, it's only fair to warn you that there's a large group of rebels marching on Baraka. They're still some way off, but it looks as though they'll arrive there about the same time as us. If this happens, it means we have to vacate this tin can in record time and help to repulse the attack.'

He noted some nervous expressions. 'Don't worry, it may never happen. They might change their minds halfway. Okay, pick up your goodies and start boarding this heap.'

A fat Belgian, scantily dressed in a pair of oil-smudged shorts and sandals, came aboard. Once the stores and the mercenaries' personal kit was stowed below, he waved a badly chewed cigar at Ford and made his way through the milling mercenaries to the wheelhouse. Ten minutes later the *Rachelle*'s engines coughed into action and the boat chugged her way to open waters.

As Albertville receded aft, a Swift took up position ahead of the *Rachelle* and commenced her escort duties. Morgan and Bream sat cramped up next to each other on a covered hatch near the bow. They considered themselves lucky in finding somewhere to sit as many of the mercenaries were still searching for places. Morgan offered Bream a cigarette. As Morgan gave him a light, he studied the three ANC soldiers huddled around a .30 Browning machine-gun, mounted in the bow.

'Are we expecting trouble on the trip itself?' he asked.

'I doubt it,' said Morgan, flicking the spent match over the side. 'The fun will probably begin when we get to Baraka.'

Eventually the men settled down for the long haul to Baraka. Suddenly the peace was abruptly shattered by the sharp crack of a rifle shot. The boat was in a turmoil as everybody jumped up, intently interested in discovering what had happened. A barrage of excited shouts rose from the aft of the *Rachelle*.

'Hey! It's that guy Marralich,' cried a voice.

Bream pricked up his ears. The name had a familiar ring. He remembered that Marralich was one of the men whom he had helped in Base HQ yesterday.

'He's gone and shot himself,' yelled someone else.

Bream groaned. No wonder Marralich was so particular about completing the beneficiary section of the contract.

'Where is he?' shouted Ford as he made his way quickly to the rear of the boat.

'In the sea. The bloke sat on the rail, stuck the barrel of his FN in his mouth and pulled the trigger. Fair blew his head off. Just like that I mean, what a crazy thing to do,' exclaimed a shaken mercenary in an excitable voice that carried around the deck.

The Belgian cut his engines, but Ford told him to start them again. 'We haven't got time to ponce around here,' he ejaculated angrily. 'Our first loyalties are to the boys in Baraka.'

Morgan sat down again on the hatch cover. 'Our first casualty and we haven't even been in action,' he commented. 'Well, someone down south don't know it yet, but he or she has just come into £7,000.'

'You reckon the Congolese Government will pay out death money in the case of Marralich? After all, he did commit suicide. No question about it,' said Bream, shocked at the grim turn of events.

'It's only us who know it was suicide, nobody else. It'll be kept in the family. You can bet your boots on that.'

Bream thought of Marralich's daughter who was the sole beneficiary. 'Thank God for that,' he reflected.

'What did you say, Tim?'

'Oh, nothing. Nothing at all.'

He lapsed into silence, smoking his cigarette.

The *Rachelle* continued chugging up the coastline and the men on board her sweltered under the heat of the pitiless sun. Some mercenaries tried escaping from the glare by sheltering in the hold, while others bunched together in miserly shadow cast by the wheelhouse. Bream and Morgan with Marvin's help tied two ropes on the rail and fixed the other ends to the hatch top. They then stretched two blankets over the ropes to form a crude refuge before crawling inside it. Their ingenuity did not pass unnoticed. Within minutes a multitude of blanket shelters sprang up around the deck.

At 18:00 hours Lieutenant Ford arranged for compo rations to be distributed from the ship's store. Although the evening meal consisted of hard biscuits and jam, the men ate with relish, dipping the biscuits into water drawn from the lake to soften them. The heat of the day was diminishing now that the cool shades of evening crept in and, as the sky turned to a deep purplish hue, the *Rachelle* passengers felt more relaxed. They talked quietly among themselves, the main topics being Marralich's suicide and the welcome they might receive at Baraka the next day. It was late evening by the time conversation ceased and cigarettes were extinguished as they settled down for the night on the open deck. Somewhere on the starboard side, a P-boat slipped by in the night, also heading for Baraka.

Toby Ashton was among the crew of three. In common with the other naval recruits, his training ceased at Albertville soon after Chase had received news of the impending attack. A quick lesson on the P-boats .50 Browning, a few practice rounds fired across the bay, and he too was on his way to Baraka. He watched the dimly-lit *Rachelle* fall behind and felt the cooling spray on his face as the P-boat surged through the water. He also wondered what tomorrow might bring.

At 5 Commando Headquarters in Albertville, Radcliffe suggested to Brogan that he should take some food to the prison. Brogan had already decided to let Dryden and Theron suffer until breakfast next morning, but Radcliffe's suggestion was too pointed to be ignored. He went to the cookhouse, collected two dixies of cold porridge and reluctantly drove up to the prison.

He rolled up by the grim walls and stopped. He picked up the two dixies and walked towards the small door which formed part of the prison gates. The two-armed Congolese guards on duty outside the gates recognised him from previous visits. One of them called through the barred slit to another guard inside the gate to open the door. A key turned in the lock and Brogan stepped inside and proceeded to the solitary cells. The same guard who had let him into the prison unlocked the first cell door and pulled the handle. Brogan peered into the dim interior. He saw Dryden and Theron huddled up on the filthy cell floor moaning softly.

'What the hell's up with you two?' he demanded, holding out the dixies of cold porridge.

They hauled themselves painfully to their feet and staggered over to him. Brogan thrust the dixies at their stomachs. They took the food with subservient overtones.

'Sergeant,' pined Theron, hugging his dixie. 'These guards keep on beating us up.' A pleading look filled his dull eyes. 'You've got to get us out of here, Sergeant. They're killing us!'

Brogan glanced at the guard and spoke to him in French. 'These prisoners tell me that they've been beaten up. Is this true?'

The guard, smelling heavily of drink, admitted the fact. He watched suspiciously as Brogan felt inside his pocket. His eyes widened when Brogan pulled out a roll of Congolese banknotes in a casual manner. Brogan peeled off a one thousand-franc note and stuffed it into the now startled guard's vest, pocket. 'Good,' said Brogan. He jerked his head at the two whimpering prisoners. 'Now go in there and fuck them up again.'

With that he turned on his heels and walked off, leaving Theron and Dryden to the mercy of the Congolese guard. He heard the thud of a rifle butt on flesh, followed by a sobbing yelp as he neared the door in the prison gates. The door closed behind him and he strolled across to his jeep.

Brogan sat in the jeep for a while, grinning.

'That'll teach the bastards,' he muttered finally. He reversed the jeep and drove slowly down the winding road to the town below.

CHAPTER TEN

The morning stars seemed to wink sleepily as the dawn peeped shyly over the eastern horizon. She blushed, reddening the skyline, and stretched her crimson fingers across the mottled heavens to wipe away the night.

Down below on the brightening waters of Lake Tanganyika the *Rachelle* thumped her way to Baraka, her vibrating engine jogging the men awake from their cramped positions on her deck. Coke bottles with strings attached to the necks plummeted into the lake and then pulled up on deck, containing enough water for shaving purposes.

Afterwards the mercenaries ate a breakfast of margarine spread on hard biscuits which was washed down with water drawn from the lake. The morning dragged on, the sun rose to its zenith and again the mercenaries sweltered on the hot deck. By early afternoon their stomachs rumbled for more food, but none was forthcoming. Instead, Lieutenant Ford issued a bottle of locally produced beer to each man.

'Is this all we get for lunch?' asked a mercenary.

'Count yourself lucky in getting a beer which should be part of the Baraka rations,' admonished Ford.

A burst of machine-gun fire rattled from the Swift escorting the *Rachelle*.

'What's that Swift doing?' enquired Bream.

'Clearing her guns,' replied Morgan. 'We must be nearing Baraka.' He directed Bream's attention to the green undulating coastline. 'You see where the land swings out,' Bream nodded. 'That's the neck of the peninsula. I think we have to sail right around the end of the peninsula and double back a few miles before we reach Baraka. It's actually across the bay from the peninsula.'

The Congolese soldiers in the bow pivoted their .30 Browning to port and kept a watchful eye on the peninsula.

'I suppose this is where we start earning our danger money,' said Bream checking the firing mechanism of his FN rifle.

'That's no lie,' grunted Morgan. He looked at his watch: 15:30 hours.

The *Rachelle* chugged on, altering course slightly to starboard. The Belgian skipper wasn't taking any chances. He meant to leave plenty of water between his ship and the coastline.

Ford also checked the time. A worried frown creased his forehead. He moved through the groups of men who were giving their weapons a last minute clean and stepped into the wheelhouse. 'Can't you get this tub to move faster?' he said to the Belgian skipper.

The skipper glowered at him. He removed an unlit cigar from his mouth and shook his head.

'You want the engine to jump out?' he demanded. 'We are travelling at maximum speed as it is.'

'Hell, I could walk faster,' muttered Ford, retreating from the wheelhouse.

Far ahead of the *Rachelle*, the P-boat with Ashton on board had already rounded the tip of the peninsula and was bearing down on the Baraka at a rate of knots. Another P-boat sped along in front, having arrived in the bay minutes before. Both had been beaten by a lumbering grey-painted trawler, bristling with heavy machine guns on her superstructure. Ashton came to the conclusion that she must be *Le Ermens*. Sergeant Fraser, Ashton's skipper, confirmed his belief. 'She must have been hiding on the other side of the peninsula to get here so fast,' he said with a chuckle.

A helicopter flew across the bay from the direction of Albertville and hovered above the converted trawler. Suddenly it hived off towards Baraka which lay by the shore away in the distance. Fraser, his hands steady on the P-boat's wheel, glanced at Ashton and Jennings, a mercenary veteran who completed the crew of three. 'I'm proposing to move in shore a bit. There's a 12.7 situated somewhere on that fourth ridge.' Ashton hastily counted the bushy green hills which sloped shoreward from his left. 'I'm expecting that gun to open up the moment the *Rachelle* pokes her nose into the bay, so keep a good lookout,' he warned.

Jennings radioed *Le Ermens* regarding their intentions and Fraser steered a course from the mainland. He cut the engines when they were about four hundred yards from the shore, and let the P-boat drift.

'Now what?' enquired Ashton from his position behind the .50 Browning in the bows.

'Now we wait,' came the reply.

Shortly afterwards the *Rachelle* edged coyly into the bay with her Swift escort. A machine gun opened up from the near peninsula tip, but the Swift quickly moved in with answering fire and silenced it.

'My God!' exclaimed Ashton in surprise. 'There's rebels on the peninsula too.'

'Not many. They're just nuisance value,' assured Fraser. 'We're after the big boys on that ridge. It rarely fails to give a hostile welcome to the *Rachelle*, or *Ruandi* when they call in here.'

'Are you telling me in all seriousness that nobody has managed to put it out of action yet?'

'That's right, even the aircraft can't pin-point its position,' put in Jennings 'The rebs bank away with the 12.7 until their position gets too hot and then they disappear with it somewhere. But they always seem to return when the next ship sails in.'

Ashton sniffed disdainfully and turned his whole attention on the all-important fourth ridge. The more he studied it, the more he realised why 5 Commando and the Air Force had difficulty in detecting the 12.7 heavy machine-gun. The ridge, like the other ridges along the coastline, could camouflage an army let alone a single gun crew. Taking a deep breath, he wrapped his hands about the Browning's twin handles and squinted through the gunsight. He straightened up scarcely believing his own eyes on seeing a stream of tracer bullets wing out from near the top of the ridge.

'Get that gun working, you bloody nitwit!' yelled Fraser. 'That's your target.'

He recovered his composure and fired a short burst towards the area but was disappointed to see that the 12.7 was still pumping out a lethal rain of bullets. Ashton quickly adjusted his aim and fired again. This time with more success.

'That's right,' he heard Fraser say. 'Now plaster that part of the ridge for all you're worth.'

Brass cartridge cases clattered about, his feet, as he fired six short bursts at the ridge. The head-splitting din from the .50 Browning made him think his eardrums would disintegrate at any moment. Ashton squeezed the trigger again and was elated see that the 12.7 had stopped firing. He relaxed his grip on the twin handles and turned around, smiling.

'For Christ's sake, don't stop now!' screamed Fraser.

His shrill warning coincided with the 12.7 opening up on the *Rachelle* once more. Ashton cursed his own stupidity and brought his .50 Browning back into action. He peppered the ridge with a long burst, ably assisted by the Swift's firepower. Under the cover of this counter-barrage the *Rachelle* slipped through the bay waters, rounded the superstructure of a sunken ship, and berthed alongside a makeshift jetty built of floating oil drums tied together and topped with planks.

From his position on the deck, Bream glimpsed two small mud huts hard by the tiny beach and a track leading up to a cluster of houses in the distance which were partly obscured by huge mango trees. To everybody's consternation, three mortar bombs hit the beach in quick succession, exploding with terrifying force. The mercenaries on the *Rachelle* hurriedly ducked down to escape the deadly fragments of white-hot metal which zipped over the ship.

Ford was the first one on his feet, a rifle in his hand.

'Come on!' he bawled to the crouching mercenaries. 'Get off this ship and up the track before the next lot of 81s arrive. Now move and move fast!'

Bream picked himself up and followed Morgan and the other mercenaries off the *Rachelle*. The planks bounced alarmingly beneath his feet as he jumped on to the crude jetty. He managed to keep his balance and, grasping his rifle, he ran along the jetty to the beach.

A fast-moving jeep with Commandant Morley at the wheel came down the track. He dropped the jeep into low gear and raced on to the sandy beach. He braked hard by the jetty, leaped out and grabbed the nearest mercenary by the arm. 'Where's Lieutenant Ford?!'

The mercenary slithered to a halt. 'Still on board, sir,' he gasped.

Morley released his grip and motioned him on with a flap of his hand. He reached the ship just as the last man jumped down. It was Ford.

'You've made it in time, Lieutenant. The rebels have just started shelling us from the Mission. Drive up with me to Ops HQ and we'll get your men into position.'

They hurried to the jeep and Morley drove like fury passed the new arrivals who were strung out along the track and running fit to bust. He turned into a tumbledown courtyard a few yards from where the track merged into what remained of Baraka's main street. A flurry of dust engulfed the jeep as Morley stamped hard on the brakes. Within seconds Ford found himself being ushered into the battle-scarred villa which served as 5 Commando's operational headquarters. There, Ford met Machine-g Heever who was commanding Baraka before Morley's recent arrival by helicopter.

'Great to see you again, Ken,' greeted Heever, warmly shaking Ford's hand.

'Forget the formalities,' cut in Morley, producing a hand-drawn map of the area. 'Let's get down to business.' They gathered around him as he spread the map out on a table that was covered in dust and specks of plaster. 'We can assume that the Simba column have now made contact with their advanced party,' said Morley. 'I should think they'll launch their main attack within the hour. Machine-g Heever here tells me that Baraka has been under fire for the last thirty minutes. He has already called up an air strike, but meanwhile you must get busy in dispersing your men along our defences.'

'Where do you think they'll be needed the most?'

'Up this end of Baraka,' answered Morley. 'String them out in the bunkers and defences from the NCO quarters, along in front of the volunteers' cookhouse, to this place. This is the part where I'm expecting the brunt of the attack.'

Ford left the villa and called over the first batch of mercenaries to arrive at Ops HQ. John Marvin, promoted to sergeant by Morley in Albertville, was among them. Ford instructed him to allocate positions between the six bunkers dug in line on the right of the T-junction where Baraka's dirt main street intersected the track from the beach. Marvin, demobilised from the Royal Engineers only two months before, soon had his charges doubling to their respective defence positions.

Morgan came up the track with Bream close behind. Ford waved him over and told him to collect the remaining arrivals and spread them out in the bunkers and behind the barricade on the left of the T-Junction. After telling Bream to stay with him, Morgan grouped his party together and took them along the street. He directed them to their firing positions within minutes, leaving only Bream and himself to find a place.

A solid bang reached their ears from the direction of a ruined Roman Catholic mission, situated just over a mile away from the centre of town. In no time at all a 75-gun shell from a Chinese-made recoilless rifle screeched over the defences. It exploded noisily in the waste ground at the rear of the volunteers' quarters. Morgan pushed Bream against a fallen tree trunk which served as part of the barricade. 'We'll stay here,' he said, cocking his FN and leaning it against the tree trunk.

A few yards away, a mercenary with his beret perched precariously on the back of his head looked across. He smiled broadly on recognising Morgan. 'Swipe me if it isn't Roy Morgan,' he said.

Morgan's head darted around on hearing his name. 'Jack Davis!' he exclaimed delightedly. 'How long have you been up here?'

'Three weeks ago, with the first batch. I see you've been promoted,' replied Davis, observing the silver star on Morgan's epaulettes. 'Pay me a visit sometime and we can celebrate Morley's mistake.'

'Where are you billeted?'

'At the back of that smashed-up building next to the Cavalry Club. Davis jerked his thumb towards a tin-roofed bungalow that had been partly demolished by shellfire. 'We call it The Hole-In-The-Wall Club for obvious reasons. No doubt we'll all be on standby tonight but come across tomorrow evening if we're still here and we'll sink a few pints. Okay?'

'Sure thing but where and what's the Cavalry Club?' queried Morgan.

Davis pointed to a grubby blue building on his right. 'Force Jumbo's quarters where the Ferret car crews hang out. There were six Ferret cars once upon a time, but now there's just four. A couple of bazooka shells did away with the other two.'

Bream flashed a look at the blue building. 'I can't see any Ferret cars,' he said.

'They're in position down the road,' said Davis. The sun was westering fast as he spoke. He noticed the shadows deepening on the hillsides. 'If the rebels intend attacking I hope they do it soon, otherwise it'll be too dark to see 'em,' he commented. 'By the way Roy,' continued Davis, 'John Vivian's here. He's heading up Force Tiger.'

A mortar barked from the bush and the ground in front of their part of the barricade erupted, spattering Bream and Morgan with earth and twigs. Another mortar boomed away some six hundred yards from the defences down the road.

'Shouldn't be long now,' Bream heard Davis say.

The day was still warm, yet he found himself shivering. He gripped the stock of his rifle, his eyes searching the bush in front of him. He thought he saw something move but put it down to his imagination. Then he blinked hard and had a second look. He was just in time to see a group of black figures disappear behind some scrub less than three hundred yards away. Bream's mouth went dry. 'They're there, Roy,' he whispered harshly. 'They're there. I swear it.'

Morgan leaned forward, rifle at the ready.

'Christ. You're right Tim,' he said, pushing his safety catch forward.

They weren't the only ones to see the rebels flitting through the bush.

'Hold your fire, men!' shouted someone whose voice sounded distinctly like Morley's. Bream glanced quickly to his rear. It was Morley all right. The commandant was standing in the middle of the road with a revolver tucked in his belt, apparently oblivious to his lack of cover.

'Start shooting only when you hear my whistle. Not before!' he enjoined clearly without a trace of nervousness. Heever approached him armed with a light machine-gun. 'Check with SM Riley in the radio room whether Bravo is on the way. If we don't get an air strike within thirty minutes we can forget about it.'

Heever dashed to the radio room, housed in close proximity to the villa. Morley pulled out his whistle and put the mouthpiece between his teeth. Without a flicker of emotion, he watched the rebels creeping nearer under a sporadic barrage of mortar fire.

'Advance!' screamed a rebel from the bush.

The sound of Morley's whistle pierced the air.

As one, the men in the bunkers and behind the barricades opened up with all available weapons. The air about the defences seemed to thump and bounce as the combined firepower roared out a deadly defiance at the rebels. Gripped in the terrifying moment of battle, Bream squeezed round after round into the bush. He could see them clearly now as they flitted among the sparse scrub. The next instant the rebels had broken cover, racing through the grass on the defence perimeter. Then Bream caught sight of two rebels being flung backwards by the force of Morgan's bullets.

That was all that Bream had time to see. The next instant a rebel came leaping towards him, firing short bursts from the hip with a Chinese burp gun. Trance-like, Bream fired back and was rewarded by the sight of the man jumping into the air and pitching sideways into the long grass.

'I got him,' mumbled Bream, a peculiar feeling sweeping over him. He cuddled his rifle butt to his cheek as more rebels rushed towards him brandishing guns and chanting wildly.

'Oh, mother,' he thought, taking aim at the nearest rebel.

Garrity, the Cuban pilot, swept his B26 fighter-bomber low across the coastline, pouring on the revs for all he was worth. He knew he must fly to Baraka and back to the airfield before dark, otherwise he would be in dire straits. Albertville Airport was not equipped for night flying. A fact which Garrity knew only too well. His aircraft was responding excellently, despite its full quota of rockets and belts of ammunition to feed the eight machine-guns in the B26's nose. He kept the aircraft in level flight and pin-pointed his position from familiar landmarks on the coast before switching on his intercom.

'Bravo to Queen, Bravo to Queen,' he repeated.

SM Riley's voice came through Garrity's earphones.

'Queen to Bravo. Am reading you four-by-five. Over.'

'Bravo to Queen I am ten minutes from your position. Please advise where I should attack. Over.'

A different voice came crackling through the ether.

'Bravo this is Sunray speaking. I repeat, this is *Sunray.*' Garrity wrinkled his nose thoughtfully. Things must be pretty bad if Morley wants to speak to him personally, he surmised.

'Go ahead, Sunray,' he said.

'Attack along the whole length, sixty yards from our defences,' instructed Morley.

The bay unfolded below the Cuban and he saw the ragged buildings of Baraka on his left. He also saw the flickering flashes of gunfire.

'Bravo to Sunray I read you clearly. Roger. Roger and out.'

He armed the rockets in the pods beneath the B26 wings and swung the control stick to port. He brought the aircraft back on even keel and then went into a shallow dive as he flew parallel with 5 Commando's defences.

The mercenaries watched with happy relief as Garrity brought his fearsome armoury into action. It was the first time in Bream's life that he had witnessed eight .50 Brownings firing simultaneously. The noise was deafening, reminiscent to that of a calico being ripped apart, but magnified ten thousand times. The scrub flew in all directions under Garrity's strafing, the sound mingling with the screams of terrified and badly maimed men. The B26 gained height at the end of the defences, circled in the sky and roared in again. This time Garrity fired his rockets in quick succession with telling effect. He pulled on his control stick and glanced back at the trail of terror and destruction he had wrought in front of the defences.

Judging from the mercenaries standing on the barricades and waving to him, he guessed that he had done a good job. He gave himself a congratulatory smile before calling up Baraka's radio station. 'Bravo to Queen. No time for another strike but will patrol over your position 06:30 hours tomorrow. Over.'

Morley came on the intercom. 'Sunray to Bravo. Well done and thank you. Over and out.'

Garrity waggled the B26 wings as a farewell gesture and then set course for Albertville, leaving behind a group of very happy men and a bloodied rebel army.

CHAPTER ELEVEN

Garrity was as good as his word. At 06:30 hours prompt, he flew his B26 low over Baraka accompanied by two T-28 aircraft. He saw platoons of mercenaries below him fanning out in the bush outside the perimeter, combing the undergrowth for dead and disabled rebels. He contacted the Baraka radio station to enquire whether they could present him with a target. The reply was negative. The Simbas had lost heart after his air strike and had retreated to the hills. The news disappointed Garrity and the two other pilots, particularly in the pocket. Obviously, no bonus money was forthcoming from the Baraka combat area and so they headed for home, promising to return later in the day.

Bream was among the men searching the bush. He felt extremely tired having been on guard all night. His curiosity, however, compensated for his lack of energy as he trampled through the scrub. He had already found five dead rebels when he chose to look under a small thorn tree. There, unexpectedly, he discovered a rebel still alive although suffering terribly from a gaping stomach wound.

The rebel gazed up at Bream with pain-filled eyes. No longer a weapon-waving, yelling Simba high on dagga – just a badly wounded and helpless human being. Bream stared at him, wondering what he should do. The rebel stared back from the ground. He gave out a low moan that clawed at Bream's sympathy. Somewhere in the distance a rifle shot rang out. Bream flinched. He looked to his right and saw Morgan stooping over a dead rebel. Bream decided to ask his advice.

'Roy,' he called. 'We've got a live one here.'

'Shoot him', said Morgan, standing up and sliding something into his trouser pocket.

'Shoot him?' gulped Bream in bewilderment. 'I don't think you understand me, Roy. The man's harmless. He's wounded!' Morgan's eyebrows lifted fractionally. He strolled over to Bream and looked down at the badly wounded prisoner.

'Now let me get this straight,' he said to Bream. 'You don't want to shoot him, because he's hurt. Correct?'

'That's about it.'

'Well, I got news for you, pal. He wouldn't hesitate to do you in if you were captured alive. Now give me elbow room.' Morgan raised his rifle and squeezed the trigger. The rebel's head jerked against the ground. Morgan lowered his FN and gave Bream a pitying glance. 'He was half dead anyway. What's more, Tim, civilisation ceased the moment, you landed at Albertville Airport, try to accept, that fact.'

'All I can say, it's going to be a damned long time before I do accept it.'

'It took me a long time too, until I saw what these bastards are capable of.'

Bream did not reply but continued staring at the body. Morgan gave him a gentle shove. 'Search him. You never know what you might, find.' He patted his trouser pocket. 'I've found eleven thousand francs already.' Bream felt sick. Noticing his reaction, Morgan went personally to the body and rummaged through the clothing. With a satisfied grunt he pulled out three bloodstained one thousand-franc notes from the rebel's left tunic pocket. He thrust, them into Bream's reluctant hand. 'There you are,' he said. 'Your first bit of loot.'

Giving Bream an encouraging pat on the back, Morgan walked off to carry on his own search for bodies. Bream let the soiled notes flutter from his hand.

Marvin was one of the few mercenaries not engaged in the search, having been detailed with another sergeant to organise a party to offload the *Rachelle*. He collected a dozen men and marched them to the beach where he quickly got them at work. Within the hour the tiny beach was covered with stores and mercenaries personal belongings. The other sergeant, supervising the unloading from the ship, called out that the holds were cleared. Feeling rather pleased at the speed the work had been done, Marvin ordered the men to fall out for a smoke. He too lit a cigarette and sat himself down, unwittingly, in the shade of some petrol drums to enjoy it.

Before he could finish it, Ford drove on to the beach in Morley's jeep with a fellow officer in the passenger seat. They stopped by Marvin. He stood up, crushing the cigarette.

'Have you completed unloading the ship?' asked Ford.

'Yes, sir. About five minutes ago.'

'That's fine. Now come with Lieutenant Craven and me to Kontonka. We want some help to shift the dead rebels. You can leave this works detail under Sergeant Jooster's command.'

'Kontonka, sir?' queried Marvin.

'It's the name of the Congolese village down the end of Baraka. Jump into the back, Sergeant, and we'll be on our way.'

'Hang on a minute Ken,' said Craven to Ford, hopping off the jeep. 'Let me tell Jooste to organise a truck for all this gear here.'

'What the hell for? Jooste has enough brains to get a truck down here.'

'Maybe, but I want it down here now. There's too much kit lying about, including a crate of Scotch. If that disappears, Morley'll have my guts for a necktie.'

'Why?'

'It's his. He told me to look out for it when he knew we were coming to the beach.'

'Oh, all right,' grumbled Ford, 'but hurry up.'

Craven returned with a triumphant grin on his face. 'All fixed up,' he said happily. 'Let's go.'

Ford took the jeep off the beach and back on the track. He turned right at the top of the track and motored along Baraka's excuse for a main street to Kontonka. As the three mercenaries entered the village, they passed a Ferret car diligently patrolling the area. Marvin found the motley collection of shanty houses and their inhabitants interesting, especially seeing how hard the Congolese women worked while their menfolk lazed around in the sun. A crowd of smiling and chanting villagers ran to the jeep when Ford drew up by the only European-type one-storey house in Kontonka.

'These people seem pretty glad to see us,' Marvin remarked.

Ford laughed. 'So, they should be. Half of them are refugees from the rebels. They know what their fate will be if Baraka falls.' He studied the smiling faces with suspicion. 'Keep a close eye on them when we're in the chief's house, Sergeant,' he said. 'I want to return this jeep to Commandant Morley with the wheels still on it.'

Marvin perched his rifle across his knees and pulled out a pack of cigarettes as the mercenary officers went in. The predominately male crowd pressed forward, their hands cupped. Marvin frowned. He looked at them and then at his cigarettes. He decided against smoking and pocketed the pack. The crowd took the hint and the begging hands vanished. Marvin struck a mute pose until Ford and Craven appeared on the steps of the house with a grey bearded old man between them. Judging from the impressive medallion on the chain around his neck, Marvin assumed that he was the local chief. The crowd started chanting in unison, confirming his opinion. The chanting, however, decreased and faded out completely as Craven spoke to them in Swahili. As he talked, the mercenary officer pointed to various able-bodied men in the crowd and mustered them to one side. When he had thirty lined up, he turned to Marvin. 'Walk this bunch back to camp and take them to SM Webb of the military police. He hangs out, in the shack opposite the track by Ops HQ. He's expecting them and knows what to do.'

Ford and Craven shook hands with the chief as Marvin climbed from the jeep. 'See me after you've delivered these men,' said Ford getting into the vehicle with Craven.

Marvin slung his rifle over his shoulder and began shepherding his charges along the road.

SM Webb was pleased to see Marvin. 'Marvellous,' he said, surveying the burial party. 'The sooner we dispose of the corpses the better. They'll start stinking to high heaven soon.'

'How many rebels did we kill?'

'We've counted forty-six so far and only Christ knows how many wounded managed to crawl away. They're probably licking their wounds somewhere on the other side of the mission right now.'

'What mission is that?'

'Where the priest of Baraka used to live. You find these types of missions in most Congolese towns. This one's about, a mile away. In fact, you can just see the roof of it from here.' Webb directed Marvin's eyes towards the hills. He glimpsed the red roof which just showed above the scrub.

'Not much there.'

'When you get up to it, it looks like the ruins old Cromwell knocked about a bit. The mission is shot full of holes with nothing inside. The desks from the schoolroom, for example, are in the volunteers' cookhouse. We send patrols to the place occasionally. Sometimes the rebels move in for a short time and shell us. We fire back and they move out damned fast, and so it goes on.'

'Why don't we capture it permanently?'

'Not worth the trouble. It would mean sending supplies to the boys holding the place and the track leading to it is perfect for ambushes. Now that you guys have arrived, Commandant Morley might have fighting patrols going to it fairly regularly. When that happens, the rebels will think twice about going there, then we shan't be troubled with their lousy shelling anymore.'

'I can't understand how we only killed forty-six yesterday,' said Marvin. 'I would have sworn that Bravo knocked that many off alone.'

'The darkness came down too soon. The light was pretty deceiving, but I reckon there are more bodies somewhere in the bush. Uncanny how we got off so lightly. Hope it's an omen for the rest of the contract.' Webb looked up at the sun. 'I better get this burial party in action. I'll see you later.'

'I've got to report to Lieutenant Ford. Have you any idea where he would be?'

'Try the officers' quarters next to Ops HQ,' said Webb helpfully.

Webb's guess was right. Marvin discovered Ford talking to Morgan. He broke off the conversation and smiled a welcome.

'Made it back then. Any of them try to sneak off on the way?' Ford asked with a chuckle.

'My FN put 'em off. They're Sergeant Major Webb's responsibility now.'

'That's fine, now park your body on my tin trunk and listen to me,' said Ford throwing him a cigarette. Morgan was already smoking. Marvin leaned his rifle against Ford's bed and made himself comfortable on the metal trunk. 'This is the picture,' enjoined Ford. 'At full strength, 5 Commando has seven forces. They are Force Lion, Tiger, Cheetah, Jumbo, Wildcat, Leopard and Panther. Force Panther, by the way, is Ops

HQ staff. Commandant Morley has given me Force Leopard, but there is, as Morgan already knows, one big snag.'

'And what is that?'

'Force Leopard exists in name only,' grinned Ford. 'To be more explicit, you and Morgan will be my NCOs, and I need your help to choose twenty-two volunteers from the batch which arrived on the *Rachelle*. The strength of my force being a total of twenty-five men, including we three. Morgan knows the type of soldier I want, and that type excludes any pot smokers or heavy drinkers. They're death to any force, so choose carefully. They've got to be fit, too. We've been picked for a night patrol tomorrow night and things could turn out rough.'

'Just our luck,' grumbled Morgan.

'Exactly my sentiments,' said Ford, 'but that's the way it is. Which reminds me, we want a good medic and a radio operator.'

'I saw a bloke on the *Rachelle* who was a radio operator when I was last in the Congo,' put in Morgan. 'I'll grab him for us before Riley gets any ideas about having him for Force Panther.'

'That's okay by me,' agreed Ford. 'What's his name?'

'Ames, I think.'

The mercenary officer scribbled Ames's name on a scrap of paper. 'Look, you track down Ames and round up the rest of the boys. Once you've done that, get yourself meal. It should be at least lunchtime by then.'

'I should think it will be,' flashed Morgan in mock despair.

'What do you want me to do if Sergeant Morgan's going to do all that?' asked Marvin.

'Find a medic,' answered Ford. 'There should be a special list next door in Ops HQ on men who have a trade or a profession which could be of use to 5 Commando.'

'I'll get cracking on trying to track down Ames and the rest of the boys we want,' said Morgan. 'Otherwise, I won't, eat today.'

'Good idea.' Ford turned to Marvin. 'You stay here until I've checked that list for a medic.'

Ford was soon back.

'Any luck?' Marvin asked him.

'I think so. A guy by the name of Tully. Medics are pretty rare birds up here, so start looking for him right away.'

Marvin left the officers' quarters, wondering where he should begin his search. Quite a few men who were no longer on duty passed Marvin on their way to the volunteers' cookhouse for an early lunch. He decided to try there before anywhere else.

He walked by a row of rebel corpses awaiting burial and took a short cut between the officers' mess and the volunteers' quarters to the cookhouse. He went inside and shouted for Tully in his best British Army voice.

A gawky youth, his hair cut shorter than the bristles on a toothbrush, stood up at the back of the spacious room. 'I'm Tully,' he called.

Marvin signal led him over. Tully wended his way through the eating mercenaries and stood to attention in front of Marvin. The youth looked so thin that Marvin wondered if he had the wrong man. 'There's no other Tully, is there?' he enquired hopefully.

'No, Sergeant. I'm the only one with that name as far as I know.'

'Then you must be the person who knows something about medicine.'

'That's right, Sergeant. If you count two years at medical school before a shotgun marriage interfered with my studies.'

Tully's answer surprised Marvin. He couldn't think it possible that anyone with Tully's stature would ever make first base with a woman, let alone put her in the club. Appearances were indeed deceiving.

'You a medical student and you couldn't terminate her pregnancy?' he said incredulously.

'She told me too late. It was a put-up job in the first place.'

You can say that again, thought Marvin. 'Well, Tully,' he said. 'You must have learnt something useful in those two years, besides assisting the population explosion.'

'I certainly hope so,' he replied, his face reddening with anger and embarrassment.

'So do I, because now you're medical orderly to Force Leopard and under the command of Lieutenant Ford,' rapped Marvin. 'We're on patrol tomorrow night, so make sure that you aren't on a guard roster tonight. I want you bright-eyed and bushy-tailed in case something happens.'

'Very good, Sergeant, but I'll need a medical kit.'

'See Lieutenant Ford about that after you've finished eating.' He dismissed Tully and went outside where he bumped into Morgan.

'Did you get your medic?' asked Morgan.

'You could say that. Now before I do anything else I intend having a good wash and shave, and then find a place for my kit and me,' he said, stroking his unshaven chin.

'There's a small water pump over there,' said Morgan pointing to the left of the Ferret car quarters. 'If you don't fancy that, you can always wash in the lake. As for your sleeping arrangements, I suggest you move into the NCOs' billet next to the mechanical section on the right, passed the guardroom. I'll be moving in there later if there's still room.'

Marvin had little difficulty in locating the NCOs' billet. It was a low building, devoid of windows along its front, but with two sets of double doors. He pushed open the door which had Stalag 17 scrawled on it in red paint.

'Hi' said a cheerful voice from inside the dark interior. 'Are you one of the men who arrived yesterday?'

'Dead right. I'm John Marvin. Any vacant bed spaces in here?'

'Two in this room and one through the back, but you're welcome to share this room. Grab that space over in the corner if you don't mind bats. We've got a colony of the little bastards in the rafters, but they're perfectly harmless. My name is Denis Smith of Force Tiger.'

'Glad to know you. Can you reserve that corner area for me and the next bed space to it for a guy called Morgan? He'll be looking in later for somewhere to sleep.'

'No trouble,' assured Smith.

'I want to go to the beach and clean myself up before bringing my kit in here.'

'Go out of the back of this building and across the helicopter landing zone. It's a short cut.'

'Thanks.'

Being an old soldier, Marvin carried his meagre washing kit on his person. He had soon spruced himself up and had a quick bathe in the lake and, after fetching the rest of his kit to the NCOs' billet, he proceeded to the sergeants' mess for a well-deserved lunch. The first thing which struck him on going through the door were the professionally drawn murals of naked curvaceous females adorning all four walls. He stopped to admire the erotic forms in charcoal, obviously drawn by a very talented artist-mercenary, before seating himself at a long table. A plate of thin stew was dumped in front of him. He helped himself to a slice of stale bread which he softened in the stew, then began spooning the unappetising meal into his mouth as only a hungry man could.

Meanwhile in Ops HQ, SM Riley presented Morley with the latest signal from Base HQ in Albertville. He read it with mounting interest.

COMMANDING OFFICER HAS OFFICIALLY RESIGNED STOP YOU TO TAKE COMAND OF 5 COMMANDO STOP OPSUD CONFIRMING STOP CONGRATULATIONS

MAJOR STOP RADCLIFFE

Morley placed the signal with unmistakable pleasure on his desk.

'Any reply, sir?' asked Riley, producing his signal pad.

'Uh, yes. Send a signal to Paradise, reading: "Thank you for congratulations – stop – advise when Machine-g Pender arrives your position – stop – also advise when remaining replacements sail for Queen".'

'Is that all, sir?'

'That's all, Sergeant Major.'

Riley saluted Morley and departed from the room. Morley went to the orderly sergeant who was seated at a table by the door. Morley handed Radcliffe's signal to him.

'Make certain my promotion goes on Part I and II Orders as soon as possible.' Morley left the orderly room and went through to his private quarters. He opened a cupboard, took out a bottle of whisky and poured himself a drink. Holding the drink carefully, he crossed to his shaving mirror above a washbasin and raised the glass. 'Here's to a profitable contract,' he said, toasting himself.

The news of Morley's promotion to major swept through Baraka. That evening, after stand-down, Morgan and Bream visited Davis's quarters at the rear of a semi-wrecked building. They found him discussing Morley's promotion with another volunteer who spoke with a very pronounced Afrikaans accent.

'Welcome to our pad,' beamed Davis, tossing two bottles of Congo beer at them. 'This is my roommate, Dan Fouche.'

'Make yourself at home,' said Fouche moving along his stretcher so that they could sit down.

'Do you guys reckon it'll make much difference to us, now Morley's CO?' asked Davis, handing Morgan a bottle opener.

'I guess that life will go on as normal if you can call this life we're leading a normal one,' interjected Fouche.

'That's no lie,' said Davis.

'Which force are you in, Roy?'

'We're both in Force Leopard under Ford,' replied Morgan.

'Ford's okay. A bit keen, but a fair guy all the same,' said Fouche.

'I hope he's okay, because we've got a night patrol ahead of us.'

'When?'

'Tomorrow night,' put in Bream.

'You poor bastards,' said Davis. 'There ain't anything worse in my books than a night patrol.'

'Why do you say that?'

'Because you're forced to keep to the paths a lot, unlike a day patrol. And the paths are favourite places for rebels to lay their AP mines.'

'AP mines…?' began Bream.

'Anti-personnel mines,' broke in Davis flatly. 'Small, round black plastic jobs with rubber tops. They're normally buried just below the surface and explode the moment you step on 'em. The best castrator in the business. If you're lucky to survive with half a ball, you can still look forward to a life of hopping around like Long John Silver.'

Fouche noted the concern on Bream's face.

'Try walking in the same footfalls as the guy in front of you. It knocks down the odds a bit.' He produced a pack of cards. 'Now let's have a good poker session. Minimum stakes One hundred francs and we'll make the maximum five thousand. All in agreement?'

'Fair enough,' said Davis, accepting Fouche's subtle hint.

'You can deal me in for a start.'

After lunch the next day, Marvin and Morgan were relaxing on their stretchers when Ford arrived on the scene.

'You blokes are fortunate in getting some shuteye before tonight's patrol,' he said. 'I've been in conference with Morley for the best part of the day. Our plans have been amended. We're now to discover whether the rebels are regrouping for another attack or returning to Kafulo. If we don't see or hear much, we can assume that they've had enough for the time being. We are to disregard the odd stray rebel. Ops HQ is only interested in the whereabouts of any big groups.'

'Damnit. I thought we'd be a fighting patrol,' spoke up Morgan. 'Not some guys pussyfooting around in the dark on a reconnaissance mission.'

'I thought you'd be disappointed, but that's the way it is. Our task is to check rebel movements. Period.'

'And if we meet up with a large group?' questioned Marvin.

'We use our savvy and duck out fast.'

'Are we taking bearers?'

'No. We won't be out that long, but we shall be taking a guide. My kit boy, Abedi, is coming with us. His knowledge of the area should be of immense help in the dark. As we're only a recce mission, the patrol will just consist of us and eight volunteers, including a medic and radio op. Less men, less noise.'

'We'll be travelling quite light then,' said Morgan.

'Just one hundred rounds per man, one GPMG and a full water bottle each. We won't be carrying compo rations, but we'll be having a full meal before we move out. We should be back in time for lunch tomorrow.'

'No breakfast?' queried Marvin.

'No breakfast,' said Ford. 'It, won't hurt you to miss one breakfast in a while.'

'How many belts of ammo are we taking for the GPMG?'

'Three. The volunteers can take turns in carrying them.'

'Not much if we run into trouble,' muttered Morgan.

'But enough to get us out of it,' said Ford. 'I'll leave you to pick the volunteers, now if John here will warn Ames and Tully,' announced Morgan, reaching for his green beret.

He went to the volunteers' quarters and found Bream diligently cleaning his rifle.

'Tim,' he began, 'only six volunteers from Leopard are needed for tonight's patrol. I've got plenty of guys to choose from, so if you like I'll leave you out. You never know, it could be a sticky patrol – if you get my meaning.'

'What are you driving at, Roy?' he said in a puzzled tone. 'Isn't the whole of the force going on this patrol?'

'No, the situation's changed since this morning. In other words, you can spend tonight kipping instead of tramping through the bush. Why not take advantage of it?'

Bream flashed him an angry glance. 'Thanks for the out,' he said bitterly, misinterpreting his friend's good intentions, 'but I'm not cleaning this gun for the sheer hell of it. What do you think I am? A bloody coward?'

'Nobody said you were, Tim,' said Morgan soothingly.

'I hope to hell that nobody does! I may get scared a couple of times, but I'm no coward. Don't think you're doing me a favour by excluding me from tonight's patrol, because you aren't! Now that you've mentioned it you had better put my name down to go.'

Morgan looked at him with a bemused expression. 'Okay, relax. I'll put you down to go.'

'What about me, Sarge?' demanded a suntanned youth who was stripped to the waist. Morgan looked at him and remembered picking him for Force Leopard the previous day. 'Couldn't help overhearing,' he said. 'I'd like to come too.'

'Hurst, isn't it?'

'That's right, Sarge.'

'And you're the one who speaks Swahili?'

Hurst nodded. 'I grew up in Kenya and could speak the lingo better than I could speak English, when I was a kid.'

'You might be a useful person on this patrol. Consider yourself included. All I need now is four more men.'

'There's four members of Leopard in that corner playing cards,' said Hurst, pointing to them.

'Good. Now you two guys had better come across with me so that I can brief you all together,' suggested Morgan.

The card players glanced up on recognising Morgan. He noticed among them a powerfully built man who towered above the others by a clear six inches. Without hesitation Morgan decided to make him the machine-gunner of Force Leopard. It needed someone of that physique to lug a heavy GPMG over the hills outside Baraka. After some furious thinking he remembered the big mercenary's name. 'Hamilton,' he said. 'Can you operate a GPMG?'

'LMG, bazooka, GPMG – I'm familiar with 'em all, Sarge,' he replied confidently. 'I was one of the first contract boys. Kamina and Stanleyville.'

'Okay. You're the machine-gunner on tonight's patrol.'

'You three card players are going too,' he added, looking at them. Morgan turned his attention to Hamilton again. 'Make one of them your number two. You can draw the GPMG with three belts of ammunition from the armoury. The rest of you will take your FN plus one hundred rounds each. Everybody will carry one full water bottle. Make sure your water bottles are brim-full too. It's the only sustenance you'll get on this trip. An early tea is laid on in the cookhouse at 16:30 hours. Feed your faces, because you won't be eating again until noon tomorrow.'

'When do we move off?' asked Hurst who was standing behind Morgan with Bream.

'We parade outside Ops HQ at 17:30 hours.'

After being satisfied that his instructions had been understood, Morgan reported back to Ford.

'Nice work,' said Ford. 'You'd better get your kit prepared now and I'll see you on parade later.'

The parade was fully attended by those who were going on the patrol. Ford, not taking any chances, personally inspected the weapons. He then ordered everybody to dispose of any loose coins and other metallic objects that they might, have in their pockets. 'We want the least possible noise for obvious reasons,' he said by way of an explanation. Afterwards he singled out Hurst and spoke to him. 'Sergeant Morgan says that you can speak Swahili.'

'Yes, sir,' confirmed Hurst.

'My knowledge of Swahili is practically nil, so you walk behind Abedi, my kit boy. He'll be leading and I'll be behind you. He can whisper any information to you, and you can pass it straight to me. The same procedure applies should I wish to tell him something. In this way we keep any talking to a minimum.' Ford added. He fingered the butt of his holstered 9mm automatic pistol and adjusted the sling on his submachine gun. 'Time to go,' he said, signalling to Abedi.

The small patrol left Baraka, walking at an easy pace along the overgrown road which led south to Fizi. A mile down the road Abedi pointed at a faint path that vanished into the bush. Ford could see that it would ultimately take them to the hills. He nodded his agreement, and the column departed from the road. Ahead of them the sun began sinking behind the hills.

The tropical night sounds of Africa came into their own as darkness fell. The mercenaries strained their ears in an effort to detect their as yet invisible enemy, but the incessant tropical chorus, with the heavy burping of bullfrogs very much in the forefront, drowned their initial attempts. A few hours later, however, when nature's tumult receded into its proper perspective, the patrol became accustomed to the strange environment.

Ford sent word along the column to rest when they had negotiated a particularly difficult hill. Bream, in common with the rest of the patrol, sank thankfully to the ground. His breath came in laboured gasps from the exertion of the climb. It would help, he thought, if the moon overhead would shine continuously instead of disappearing behind each and every cloud. He massaged a tender kneecap that had connected hard with a jutting piece of rock in the dark. Afterwards he replenished his thirst from his water bottle and, as he drank, he vaguely wondered about what idiotic notion induced him to sign on for the Congo.

Morgan made his way to where Bream sat. 'Okay, Tim?' he asked softly.

Bream scowled. 'It wouldn't be too bad if I could see what I'm bumping into half the time. How far have we come?'

'About eight miles.'

'Is that all? It feels like eighty!'

'Shhh. Keep your voice down. Don't worry, you'll be all right once you get your second wind.'

'Jeez, I certainly hope so.'

Morgan patted his shoulder. 'You'll make it,' he assured him, rising to his feet.

Ford turned to Hurst who sat next to Abedi. 'Give him a nudge. We're moving on again.'

The ten-minute break revived their flagging spirits, and they tackled the downhill walk with more enthusiasm. Their energy waned again as they started climbing diagonally up the next hill. Ford's kit boy stopped so abruptly on rounding the hill that Hurst bumped into him. The mercenary grunted with surprise and then peered into the night.

'What's the hold up?' growled Ford on the narrow path behind Hurst.

'Your boy's seen some sort of light on the other side of the valley. If I move out the way a bit, you'll be able to see it for yourself.'

With Hurst's assistance, Ford saw a faint red glow flickering softly in the night. 'It could be a campfire. Tell Abedi to move on. We're going to investigate it.'

Hurst whispered Ford's instructions to him and Abedi increased the pace with the rest of the patrol hard on his heels. The pace was too fast for Ford's liking. The men were throwing up too much noise with their feet. 'Hurst,' he said urgently. 'Tell Abedi to cool the pace.'

Hurst had just opened his mouth to pass on the message when a brilliant crimson flash, coupled with a loud explosion, erupted beneath Abedi's bare feet. The unexpected explosion threw Ford, Morgan and Ames to the ground, but leaving Hurst, swaying precariously on his feet, his hands cupping his face. Ford's kit boy was nowhere to be seen.

The rest of the patrol stood motionless, fearing to move. Across the moonlit valley the faint red glow suddenly flared up and then vanished.

'Oh, God. Please God. I can't see, I can't see,' mumbled Hurst. He fell to his knees, gibbering like a man demented.

Ford reached for his submachine gun and scrambled to his feet. Behind him, Morgan lent Ames a helping hand who had the radio strapped to his back. The other men comprising the patrol stepped gingerly off the path as the initial shock wore off.

Ford looked back at the shaken patrol as he tried to comfort Hurst.

'Medic! Where's Tully the medic?' he called in a strained voice.

'I'm here, sir,' piped Tully nervously. He stood on the edge of the path at the rear of the column, gripping his medical kit.

'For Christ's sake, man!' exclaimed Ford. 'Get up here quickly. Hurst needs medical attention.' Tully pulled himself together and ran passed the other mercenaries to Ford. 'See what you can do for Hurst. I'm going to discover what, has happened to our guide.'

He found Abedi face downwards on the slope a few feet from the path. A thorn tree had stopped his sliding further. He lay there, barely moving. Ford's worst fears were confirmed when he shone his torch on his kit boy's legs. The right leg ended in a red jellied mess at the knee. The left leg hadn't fared much better, the flesh having peeled away up to the thigh, showing the bone. Ford hastily removed the lanyard from his shoulder and knotted it tightly above the right knee to stem the flow of blood. He then dragged Abedi on to the path.

'Need any help?' said Morgan as the mercenary officer examined Abedi's left leg.

'Get some morphine and a couple of field dressings from Tully.' Morgan walked back to Tully who was on the verge of completing the bandaging of Hurst's eyes. He drew the medical orderly aside where they exchanged some quiet words. Afterwards Tully fetched a tube of morphine and two field dressings from his medical kit which he gave to Morgan.

'How's Hurst?' asked Ford, taking the morphine from Morgan.

'Not too good according to Tully. He reckons that one eye has gone for sure, but the other one might be saved if he gets the proper medical attention in time.'

Ford gave a pessimistic grunt and broke off the top of the tube, exposing the needle. His kit boy started whimpering.

'The shock's wearing off,' said Ford, pushing the morphine needle into Abedi's arm.

'How the hell are we going to get these two back to base?' hissed Morgan.

'I don't know yet. Wrap these field dressings around Abedi's left leg while I talk to Ames.'

Ames was kneeling by the path, fiddling with his radio when Ford reached him. He glanced up at Ford with a despondent look on his face. 'Suppose you want me to raise base.'

'Yes. We must get a helicopter here for the wounded. If we contact Baraka now, we should have a helicopter here three or four hours after first light.'

'We've got two chances in raising base and they're both nil,' said Ames glumly. 'The set's gone dead. It must have smashed against a rock or something when I fell backwards.'

'Can't you mend it?'

Ames stared at him. 'Mend it?' he echoed. 'Listen to this.' He picked up the radio and shook it near Ford's ear. 'You could do the bloody cha cha to it.' Ford returned to Hurst.

'Are you capable of walking if I find someone to guide you?'

The blind mercenary put his arms out and plucked at Ford's shirtfront. 'Don't know,' he quavered. 'Can't see anything.'

'Damnit, man. How do you expect to see anything with a bandage wrapped around your eyes,' he snapped, losing his patience. Ford immediately regretted his outburst. 'Don't worry. We'll get you back to base somehow,' he added in an apologetic tone.

Somewhere across the valley a rifle shot punctured the night. Ford left Hurst and went to Morgan who was busily bandaging the Congolese kit boy's shredded left leg.

'The rebs are on to us,' commented Morgan. 'That AP mine exploding was a dead giveaway.' He stopped his bandaging and sat back on his haunches, utterly defeated by the extent of Abedi's wounds. 'It's hopeless,' he said with a grimace. 'I can't stem the flow of blood.'

Another shot echoed in the dark and a bullet smacked into the hillside further up the path.

'How many rebels do you think are out, there?' asked Ford, more to himself than to Morgan.

'Dunno. Could be anything from one to a hundred. We'll soon know if we don't shift our arses out of here pronto,' Morgan replied grimly.

'We won't be able to move very fast, not with a blind man, we can't. As for Abedi here…' Ford shrugged his shoulders, his voice trailing off as he looked at the whimpering figure of Abedi.

The Congolese lad had been with him ever since he came to Baraka and Ford had taken a great liking to him. He watched his kit boy struggle on to his side, staring at him like a helpless puppy appealing to his master. Ford averted his eyes guiltily. Attempting to carry Abedi over the rugged terrain they had traversed just didn't seem possible, especially in the dark. He couldn't visualise his kit boy lasting the trip. Conversely, he couldn't leave him for the rebels to find. Ford knew that Abedi would get a short shrift from them. What the devil should he do?

A fusillade of shots crashed out from the bottom of the valley and bullets peppered the slope above the mercenaries. Bream caught his breath.

'They're getting nearer,' Morgan announced ominously.

The small-arms fire blew a hole in Ford's mental block. His duty immediately became crystal clear. 'Sit Abedi up, give him a drink and don't let him look my way.'

Morgan was on the point of querying Ford's strange order, but he changed his mind and reached for his water bottle. Ford slipped round to Abedi's side as Morgan uncorked the water bottle. He placed it to Abedi's lips. Trying to behave as casually as possible, Ford turned his back on his kit boy and slowly withdrew his automatic pistol from the holster. He kept the gun hidden as he turned again, but his precautionary move was unnecessary.

Abedi's whole attention was centred on Morgan's water bottle. Ford knew that his opportunity had arrived. He quickly levelled the pistol a fraction above his kit boy's left ear and squeezed the trigger.

Nothing happened. Ford's jaw sagged in anguish as the awful truth thudded home. Abedi felt Morgan's hands stiffen against his back and he instinctively turned. He glimpsed the metallic glint of the pistol in Ford's hand. He screamed in fright, dropped the water bottle, and threw himself bodily down the dark slope.

'Damnit Damnit,' croaked Ford in misery. 'Forgot to cock the bloody gun.'

Morgan scrambled to his feet and ran to Hurst. He brushed Tully aside and grabbed the blinded mercenary around the waist. 'Walk in a straight line,' he commanded.

He brought Hurst up to Ford who was frantically peering down the slope. Somewhere down there Abedi was screaming something in Swahili at the top of his voice. Ford wheeled about when Morgan tapped him in the back. He saw Hurst next to Morgan, his eyes still swathed in bandages, arms outstretched. The mercenary officer felt that he owed Morgan a debt of thanks for using his initiative. He clasped Hurst's nearest arm and spoke to him. 'Hurst, can you understand what Abedi is shouting?'

'He's pleading with us not to shoot him,' said Hurst, woodenly.

'Anything else?' urged Ford.

'No,' muttered Hurst, trying to fight down the searing pain in his head.

'Tell him we won't shoot him.'

The agony Hurst was experiencing showed in his voice as he called out. The maimed kit boy answered back shrilly from the cloak of darkness which hid him.

'What the devil is he saying now?' rasped Morgan in exasperation, darting a look down the path where the rest of the men impatiently waited. Bream gripped his rifle hard as he tried to contain his fear.

'He wants us to give him a chance. He's saying that if we shoot him, he will be dead, but, if we leave him alive, he will try to evade the Simbas and make his own way back to Baraka. If he doesn't get to Baraka he will die anyway, but he would like us to give him that chance of crawling back to camp.'

'He'll bleed to death before he's crawled a hundred yards,' declared Ford.

'Look, Lieutenant,' cut in Morgan, sensitive to the patrol's restlessness. 'Let it go at that. We can't carry him, and we can't shoot him unless we waste valuable time searching for him.'

'I guess you're right,' said Ford wearily. 'Hurst, tell Abedi that I'm throwing my water bottle down to him. You can also tell him that I hope he makes it,' he added softly, knowing full well that Abedi's task was nigh on impossible.

In a flat but loud voice, Hurst, passed on Ford's message.

The mercenary officer unstrapped his water bottle and tossed it down the dark slope, hoping that it would land near his kit boy. Another volley of rifle fire crackled from the floor of the valley.

'Shall I give the boys the order to shoot back?' enquired Morgan.

Ford shook his head. 'No,' he said numbly. 'It would be a waste of good ammo. Take Hurst back to Tully and we'll start walking back. We've found out what we want to know. Those guys firing at us are just a rearguard of sorts. The main body is probably now in Kafulo.'

Morgan escorted Hurst to the medical orderly.

'I'll give Tully a hand with Hurst if it's needed,' promised Marvin, feeling very much the bystander.

Higher up the path, Ford took one last lingering look down the hillside. He then turned his back sadly on the macabre scene and wended his way down the path to join the others.

Not unexpectedly, the return journey proved to be a slow one, Ford having set the pace with Hurst in mind. The patrol entered Baraka midway through the afternoon, its morale at a low ebb. The *Rachelle* had long since sailed from the bay, but by good fortune the men spied a helicopter on the dusty landing zone. It had, an hour before their arrival, flown in Machine-g Pender at Morley's request. It was now available to take Hurst, to Albertville. Ford reported to Morley and then arranged for the evacuation of the blind mercenary. Afterwards, Ford flopped down on to his stretcher in the officers' quarters – a tired and a very dispirited man.

In the volunteers' quarters, Bream threw his backpack and unused rifle onto his stretcher. He picked up his mess tins and proceeded to the cookhouse. On his way he saw Morley going into Ops HQ in company with a machine-g whom he had not seen in Baraka before. Bream didn't give it another thought as he entered the cookhouse.

Morley poured Pender a liberal tumblerful of Scotch in his room and handed it to him. 'I'm glad you didn't have much difficulty with the Belgian pay officer in Leopoldville.'

'It went smooth as a dream,' Pender assured him. 'Radcliffe did a good job with the nominal role. The Belgian didn't suspect a thing. It was a stroke of luck you having a patrol out last night too.'

Morley chuckled. 'I don't believe in luck. Now it only remains for me to notify Radcliffe about the result.'

He pulled out a small notebook and leafed through it until he came to a page covered in groups of letters.

'Your own private code I see,' observed Pender. 'You certainly don't leave anything to chance.'

'Not if I can help it,' replied Morley, tearing out the page. He called the orderly sergeant into the room and presented it to him. 'See that this coded message is given to SM Riley personally. I want it transmitted to Lieutenant Radcliffe in Albertville immediately. Do you understand, Sergeant? Immediately.'

'I'll take it to the radio room right now, sir.'

Morley rubbed his hands in a cheerful manner when the orderly sergeant had left the room. He grinned at Pender.

'Well, that tidies up the business this end. Now it's up to Radcliffe.'

'Fine,' said Pender. 'How about pouring yourself a drink? You deserve it.'

'Yes, I do deserve it,' replied Morley, reaching for the bottle of Scotch.

CHAPTER TWELVE

The Makasi Club was not particularly full when Captain Bradley Chase walked in. He perched himself on a high stool at the small bar and watched with interest a group of Cuban pilots playing poker while he waited for someone to serve him. He had consumed a fair amount of liquor before leaving his ship and could afford to bide his time until Fletcher, duty barman for the night, finished serving a highball to a CIA man at the end of the bar. Chase ordered a cold beer. Fletcher took one from the refrigerator, prised off the cap and slid the bottle towards Chase with a glass.

'Seventy francs, please.'

Chase plonked the money down and filled the glass. He swigged the icy beer down quickly and poured the remaining beer from the bottle into his glass. In all, it had been a hectic day for him, what with reading and checking reports from the crews returning from Baraka. It was a nice change to get away from naval matters and relax in the congenial atmosphere of the Makasi Club. Working and living aboard ship after a while and the simple amenities of the club was more to his liking.

'Set up another beer,' he said to Fletcher. 'That last one went down too fast.' Chase gazed around the club. 'Any film show tonight?' he asked.

'Not tonight,' said Fletcher, swapping the empty bottle for a full one. 'Maybe tomorrow night if you're around. One of our aircraft is flying a film here from Stanleyville. It could come tomorrow.'

'Pity. I could have done with a film show this evening.'

Heads turned towards the doorway, Chase's among them, as two Congolese in European attire entered, escorted by Lagache. It was unusual to see people of Congolese nationality in the Magasi Club as they were not particularly welcomed.

If a high-ranking Congolese officer or civil servant chose to drink there his presence was endured, but that was all. The Congolese civilians with Lagache, judging from their bearing and expensive suits, held high office. In common with the majority of Europeans in the room Chase only mixed with Africans on sufferance, and he reluctantly shifted his stool to allow Lagache and his companions to get to the bar.

Lagache thanked Chase and drew the mercenary officer's attention to the Congolese civilians. 'Captain Chase, let me introduce you to Monsieur Humbert the finance minister of this province, and Monsieur Mutangi, his assistant.'

Humbert extended his hand, and Chase had no option but to shake it.

'Are you the officer in command of the navy?' he asked in impeccable English.

'Yes,' said Chase.

'I'd like you to show Monsieur Mutangi and myself your naval base sometime. I'm sure it would be a most interesting experience.'

'I'll see what I can do,' said Chase without much enthusiasm.

Lagache ordered whisky for the three of them and, as an afterthought, included Chase in the order. The drinks arrived and Lagache handed them around. 'My two guests are on a visit before flying to Elizabethville,' he explained.

'What are you here for?' Chase enquired.

'Talks with Operations-South,' interjected Mutangi.

'Financial talks?' went on Chase, angling.

Humbert laughed. 'Could be,' he said.

Chase grinned mirthlessly and dropped the subject. Inwardly, however, he was more than curious to know the reason behind Humbert's visit to Operations-South. Morley would also like to know, he reflected. He decided to try to find out. 'When you've had your drinks, I'll take you back to my ship if you're still interested. You won't be able to see much, but I can tell you a bit about the navy's operations.'

Lagache became uneasy about Chase's proposition. He was due to see Colonel Cartier within the hour. By then he hoped to have Humbert and Mutangi safely ensconced in the Hotel du Lac.

'Don't you think tomorrow morning would be better, Captain?' he said. 'The ministers have had quite a hard day and I'm sure they must be tired.'

'That is kind of you to suggest it, but now Captain Chase has afforded us the opportunity we shall be delighted to go,' replied Humbert.

Lagache was very hesitant to leave them in Chase's company, but the ministers had obviously made up their minds. He hoped that Chase would keep a civil tongue in his head, thereby sparing Op-Sud considerable embarrassment.

'As you wish,' said Lagache at length. 'No doubt Captain Chase will have a lot of things to tell you.'

'Plenty,' said Chase, spooning an ice-cube into his Scotch. He gulped down his drink and plonked the empty glass on the bar. 'I've got a car outside, so we won't have to walk,' he informed them.

'Excellent,' smiled Humbert, moving away from the bar. 'We're ready to go.'

Chase led the way. Just before the two Congolese ministers stepped into the car Lagache spoke to Humbert in French.

'I'll see you both at the hotel at breakfast time.'

'Aren't you coming with us?' asked Humbert rather amazed.

'No, unfortunately. I have an appointment, with Colonel Cartier.'

'Then breakfast it is. Thank you for your assistance, Monsieur Lagache.'

Humbert gave Lagache a friendly wave as the car drove off.

Chase parked the car outside the railway station and directed the Congolese ministers to his ship. Being somewhat short of breath from their awkward walk, they gladly accepted Chase's invitation to seat themselves in his cabin. He poured them each a large brandy and one for himself.

'It's not the best of brandies, but nevertheless it is brandy,' said Chase, knowing full well that he had a better brand stashed out of sight.

'Any drink is welcomed after that walk from the station,' declared Humbert with a grin. He held up his glass. 'Cheers, isn't it Captain?'

'That's right – cheers,' reciprocated Chase. He threw back his head and sank his brandy without any respect for the drink. He refilled his glass and sat on the edge of his bunk opposite Humbert and Mutangi.

'You certainly have a selection of drinks, Captain,' said Humbert, observing the array of liquor bottles on a nearby shelf.

'Nothing else to do in this hellhole except eat, drink, sleep and fight. I do plenty of each when given the chance.' He lounged back on his bunk and surveyed his guests. 'When do you go to Elizabethville?'

'Tomorrow afternoon,' replied Mutangi.

'Was your visit here successful?'

'Reasonably,' said Humbert.

'That's nice to hear.'

With practised ease, Chase rolled off his bunk, picked up his bottle of brandy and topped up Humbert's glass.

'Thank you, Captain.'

Chase reclined on his bunk again and cocked his head towards the finance minister. 'By the way,' he said casually. 'What was the purpose of your visit?'

Humbert looked over his glass to Chase. 'I'm afraid that's confidential.' Humbert sipped his drink and then looked at Chase again. 'How about telling us something about the navy. I'm sure that navy's activities are far more interesting than our discussions with Operations-South.'

'Well,' began Chase, feeling lightheaded from all the liquor he had consumed, 'our main purpose in life is to stop supplies reaching the rebels from the other side of the lake. We also keep the rebs on their toes by shooting up their encampments along the shore.'

'Do you suffer many casualties?' put in Mutangi.

'Not many, as my men can shoot a damn sight straighter than those black bastards we're fighting against,' he said, forgetting the company he was keeping.

Humbert and Mutangi looked at each other quickly.

'Captain,' spoke up Humbert, peevishly. 'You must, remember that we have black skins too. We should appreciate it if you would cease saying things like that.'

Chase glowered at them and helped himself to another brandy. 'You're too sensitive. I was only referring to the rebels.'

'It makes no difference,' said Humbert, hotly. 'If you were speaking about the rebels, why not say that they're rebels or Simbas or, if you wish, the Liberation Army. But never describe them in the words you have just used.'

The brandy spoke Chase's true feelings. He whirled around, drink spilling from his glass. 'Look here,' he rapped. 'When I'm on my ship

I say what the hell I like! Don't you two jumped-up monkeys dictate at me.'

Humbert leapt to his feet. 'How dare you insult us, Captain. This is our country, and you are just a hired fighter. Remember that.'

Chase threw his glass on the floor. 'Balls!' he exclaimed, glaring at them in anger. 'I'll remember nothing.'

'In that case we have no option but to report your disrespectful behaviour to higher authority.'

'Like hell you will,' roared Chase, seeing red. He dived for his bunk and whipped a .45 Colt automatic out from beneath his pillow. Humbert took a step back as Chase pointed the gun at him. Mutangi gripped the sides of his chair but remained seated. 'Nobody, but nobody, speaks to me like that,' he seethed, his mind aflame with drink.

'Put that gun away, Captain. You are making things worse for yourself.'

Chase sneered and opened his cabin door, but kept his gun trained on the two minsters. 'Guard!' he bellowed.

Footsteps sounded on the deck below.

'Coming, sir.'

'And make it fast!' shouted Chase. Mutangi began rising from his chair. 'Stay put in that chair and that applies to you too,' he said to Humbert.

'Yes, sir?' puffed a mercenary, reaching the cabin door.

'Your rifle loaded?'

'A full magazine, sir.'

'Okay, take these two to the brig. If they escape I'll have your balls for a necktie.'

'They won't escape.'

'They had better not. When you've locked them up, get hold of your guard commander and tell him to get a P-boat ready for sea. When he's done that, I want him to report to me. Now take them away.'

Humbert stopped at the doorway and looked back at Chase.

'You'll regret this when the Central Government hears about it.'

'You'll regret it before I do,' announced Chase as the guard prodded Humbert forward with his rifle.

He emptied the remaining brandy from the bottle into his glass and emptied it down his throat a moment before the guard commander arrive.

'Your P-boat is ready for sea duty, sir.'

Chase stuck his Colt .45 behind the buckle of his belt. 'Come with me to the brig, sergeant,' he said. 'I'll be needing your help.'

The two men made their way down below deck to the ship's defunct cold storage room which served as the brig. Chase swung the handle on the heavy door and ordered the two Congolese ministers to step outside. They were plainly frightened.

'What are your intentions now, Captain Chase?' asked Humbert in a low voice.

'We're going for a little sea trip.'

The guard commander walked down the *Albertville*'s gangplank, followed by the ministers, with Chase bringing up the rear. The party walked along the quay to where the P-boat lay moored. The guard commander stepped into the boat and held it steady to let the other three men board. Chase ordered Humbert and Mutangi to squat on the bottom. The guard commander started the engine and the P-boat headed through the choppy waters until they were well clear of the docks.

'Cut engines, Sergeant,' said Chase to the guard commander.

The P-boat wallowed gently on the lake.

'What now, sir?'

'Bring me two of the .50 ammo boxes from the bow. You two bastards, meanwhile, roll on to your stomachs and rest your hands behind your backs.' Chase produced a length of cord from his pocket and tied their wrists together. His intentions were now blatantly obvious.

'Mercy, Captain,' pleaded Mutangi. 'You have our word that that we won't mention the incident aboard your ship if you free us.'

Chase laughed harshly. 'Don't take me for a bloody fool or I'll make you suffer painfully.'

'Here's the ammo boxes,' grunted the guard commander, lugging the last one to the centre of the boat.

'Thanks, Sergeant,' Chase gave him some cord. 'Tie one end of this to an ammo box and the other end to this one's ankles,' he said nodding at Mutangi. 'I'll see to the other one.'

In desperation Humbert twisted his body and kicked out at Chase. The finance minister's surprise attack made Chase lose his footing on the wet deck and he fell backwards. Before Chase could scramble to his feet Humbert had struggled up and pitched himself headfirst over the side.

'The bastard! The slimy bastard!' cried Chase, drawing his Colt .45 and rushing to the side of the P-boat.

He caught sight of Humbert's head bobbing in the water not far from the boat. Chase steadied himself with his left hand on the gunwale and fired four shots in quick succession at Humbert's head. The finance minister let out a small cry and disappeared below the waves. Chase fired one more shot at the spot where Humbert had vanished and surveyed that particular stretch of water for some minutes before satisfying himself that Humbert would trouble him no more.

'I'm sure you got him,' said the guard commander as Chase checked the cord around Mutangi's ankles.

'So am I. I hope so,' added Chase.

He assisted the guard commander to wrap the loose end of the cord around the ammunition box and to tie it firmly, before clutching Mutangi beneath the armpits and hauling him part-way over the gunwale. Mutangi stuttered something and fainted in sheer terror. Totally unmoved, Chase jammed the gun barrel into the back of Mutangi's neck and pressed the trigger. Mutangi flopped into the water, still anchored to the boat by the ammunition box tied to his ankles. Chase heaved the heavy box overboard and Mutangi's body sank without trace.

'Start the engine, Sergeant, and let's get back to the ship,' said Chase. 'By the way, Sergeant…'

'Yes, sir?'

'Not a word to anyone about tonight.'

'I've forgotten already.'

'You're a wise man, Sergeant,' said Chase, lighting a cigarette. 'A very wise man.'

Lagache ate alone at his breakfast table in the Hotel du Lac. The dining room was populated heavily with Belgian officers and American advisers, but nowhere could he see Humbert and Mutangi. More puzzling, their beds had not been slept in either. He had immediately checked at the reception desk, but their room keys were still there. Nobody, including the night porter, had seen them entering the hotel. Lagache ate his breakfast in silence, hoping that the two ministers would appear soon.

Colonel Cartier came into the dining room and strolled over to Lagache's table. 'Good morning, Paul,' he said amicably. 'How are the VIPs?'

'I wish I knew!' he exclaimed worriedly. 'As I told you last night, they insisted on going with Captain Chase to his ship and it seems that they haven't returned.'

'You've checked their rooms?'

'Naturally, but their beds are undisturbed.'

'Maybe Captain Chase was too liberal with the drinks and they're sleeping it off aboard the *Albertville*.'

'That's a possibility,' mused Lagache. 'On the other hand, Chase isn't that friendly with Africans.'

'But Humbert and Mutangi aren't ordinary Africans,' Cartier reminded him.

'To complicate matters, their plane is arriving two hours earlier than planned. They're in danger of missing it if they don't show up shortly.'

'Take a drive down to the docks after your breakfast, Paul,' suggested the Colonel. 'If they're there you can bundle them into your car, pick up their luggage here, and drive straight out to the airport.'

'What happens if they're not on Chase's ship?'

'Then, Paul,' said Cartier gently. 'We'll press the panic button.'

He left Lagache and went to his own table. Lagache sipped his coffee and looked at his watch. It was later than he thought. He threw his napkin on the table and pushed his chair back. No time to lose if he was to get them on the plane.

He reached the railway station and parked his car next to Chase's vehicle, then he walked quickly through the station entrance and along the railway track to the catwalk. As he walked along the catwalk, he scrutinised the murky waters below in case they had met with an accident on their way back. Lagache was relieved not to see any bodies and he ran up the *Albertville*'s gangplank with renewed heart.

Chase was busily shaving when Lagache knocked on his cabin door. He peered bleary eyed at Lagache with one side of his face still partly covered in lather. 'What the hell do you want at this time of the day?' he growled.

'The two ministers you entertained last night are missing.'

'So?'

'It appears they didn't return to the hotel. I'm therefore checking to see whether they slept here.'

'Not on my ship they didn't,' Chase declared emphatically, honing a lethal looking cutthroat razor on a dilapidated leather strap. 'Humbert and his friend left here sometime after midnight. I think they said something about going to a shebeen in town.'

'A shebeen?'

'Yeah, a shebeen,' confirmed Chase. He tested the keen edge of his razor for sharpness before dipping it into a basin of hot water.

'Any particular one?'

Chase carefully studied his features in a mirror and applied the razor to his face. He scraped away an area of lather and rinsed the razor before answering. 'No, they didn't seem to be choosy. They just wanted to find a shebeen where they could pick up a couple of women, so you'd better try the cathouses as well.'

'You do surprise me. I thought they would have better taste.'

'Well, you know what Africans are like when they've got a few drinks inside them.'

'It still seems rather implausible,' murmured Lagache.

'I can't help what you think,' snapped Chase. 'Let's face it Lagache, it's their business if they want to whore around not mine.'

'Perhaps, but their welfare ultimately concerns Op-Sud.'

'Then you'd better lay on a good VD specialist when you find them,' said Chase sarcastically.

It was obvious that no more help was forthcoming from Chase, so he bade him good day and returned to his car. As he drove past the Hotel du Lac, he spied Colonel Cartier on the sidewalk going to Operations-South. He drew in by the curb. Cartier walked over to him.

'Any luck, Paul?'

'On the contrary, Colonel, I'm about to ask you to press the panic button.'

'They weren't aboard the *Albertville*?'

'Afraid not. According to Captain Chase, they left his ship about midnight, apparently to seek female company in one of the town's shebeens.'

'Highly unlikely for Humbert and Mutangi to do that,' mused Cartier. 'They look too respectable.'

'Exactly my sentiments, but you never can tell. I feel that we have to check out these places.'

'I hate to hazard a guess on how long that will take us, but we haven't any alternative. When does their plane leave?'

'About an hour from now.'

'I suggest you cancel their seats while I arrange for men to search the town.' Cartier frowned and scratched the bridge of his nose. A sure sign of his anxiety. 'Well,' he said, 'there will be the devil to pay if we don't find them. Keep in close contact with me during the day, Paul.'

'I will indeed, Colonel.'

Cartier walked away in a pensive mood, leaving Lagache deep in thought. He sighed and wished all manner of things on the two errant ministers before driving on to the airport.

In his cabin on the *Albertville*, Chase finished shaving. Lagache's visit had caused him some concern until he realised that it was a natural thing for the Belgian to do when the ministers failed to put in an appearance at their hotel. Even so, it was not likely that Lagache or Operations-South would give up the hunt with a stroke of a pen or a brief word. Lagache would be back. After all, reflected Chase, he was the last person to be seen with them.

'I'd better make myself scarce for the next, couple of days,' he muttered, buckling on his gun belt.

Lieutenant Olivier was preparing to pass the 5 Commando mailbag to the skipper of a Swift tied alongside the *Albertville* when he saw Chase approaching.

'Is Lieutenant Hackett taking this Swift, to Baraka?' demanded Chase.

'Yes sir.'

'Tell him he's got a passenger. Take care of the base while I'm away, Lieutenant. I should be back the day after tomorrow if all goes well.'

Chase tossed a small suitcase on to the deck of the Swift and then jumped down himself. 'Hurry up Hackett,' he shouted to the skipper. 'I want to get to Baraka on this contract, not the next one.'

Lieutenant Hackett smiled at Chase. 'We're on our way now, sir.'

He gave the order to cast off.

If Lagache had glanced seaward on the return journey from the airport, he would have seen the Swift with Chase aboard moving up Lake Tanganyika, approximately two miles from the shore, but the sight escaped him. He was more concerned in returning to Op-Sud in the shortest possible time.

The Colonel was in his office talking to Radcliffe when Lagache arrived. He barged in without waiting for Cartier's permission to enter. Both Radcliffe and Cartier looked at him in surprise.

'Good Lord, Paul,' said Cartier. 'Anyone would think that you've seen an army of rebels marching over the bridge towards Albertville.'

'I wish to God that is what I did see at the bridge.'

'What on earth do you, mean?'

'Come with me and I'll show you, Colonel.' Lagache nodded to Radcliffe. 'I think you should come too, seeing that this might involve 5 Commando.'

Lagache drove them in his car to the bridge spanning the large estuary on the airport road. He stopped the car and led them to a crowd of Congolese civilians gathered around on the shore by a small fishing trawler. The Greek skipper of the trawler stomped his way across the sand to them.

'About time you turned up,' he said angrily, gesticulating at Lagache. 'I've got a home to go to.'

'Presently, presently,' countered Lagache.

He brushed the Greek aside and led Cartier and Radcliffe through the curious assemblage. He stopped where the waters lapped the beach and pointed an accusing finger at a bundle of wet netting.

Cartier leaned forward. 'Good God!' he uttered.

'This trawler brought it up early this morning,' stated Lagache.

He shifted some of the net to let Cartier inspect more closely. 'I don't think we need to call in a pathologist to tell us how he died.'

'Not with a hole like that in his face,' retorted Cartier. His eyes met Lagache's. 'If this is how Humbert met his end, I doubt that we can hold much hope for his assistant.'

'Quite,' said Lagache sharply.

Radcliffe noticed an angry glint flare up in the Colonel's eyes. Cartier gazed once more at the body enmeshed in the fishing net.

'Captain Chase will be having another visit today,' he declared. 'For his sake, I hope he can explain his movements of last night.'

'And if he can't?' flashed Radcliffe.

'Then my dear Radcliffe,' began Cartier slowly, 'Captain Chase will find himself on the sticky end of Congolese justice.'

'Not a pretty picture.'

'No, Lieutenant,' announced Lagache. 'It isn't.'

He led the party back to his car.

CHAPTER THIRTEEN

Chase waited until the Swift edged against the floating jetty which protruded from the small beach at Baraka. He jumped awkwardly on to it, causing water to suck up between the planks. He regained his balance, slung the mailbag over his shoulder and, clutching his suitcase, made his way along the jetty to the beach where Morley stood.

'You've certainly stirred up a hornets' nest,' said Morley as Chase stepped ashore.

'What do you mean?'

'Didn't you entertain Katanga's finance minister and his deputy on board your ship?'

Morley's direct question shook him. The major obviously knew something which had yet to come to his notice. He knew Morley of old. Bluff and counter bluff was out. Chase decided it was time for straight talk.

'Okay, Simon, lay it on the line. What's Albertville found out?'

'Plenty – so it seems. The finance minister's body was fished out of the lake with a bullet hole in him. Op-Sud thinks you're the culprit.' Morley shook his head in a fatherly fashion. 'Oh, Brad, you should have known better. What made you think you could get away with it? He wasn't an ordinary African.'

'He shouldn't have been found. I meant to weigh him down, but he slipped overboard before I could do it,' Chase said vehemently, not bothering to deny the accusation.

'Well, they've found him, and we've got to get you out of the country somehow. They're baying for your blood at Albertville. Come to my HQ and we'll discuss it.'

'Okay, but I refuse to panic about it. Nobody can prove a thing.'

'Don't be too sure about that,' replied Morley.

'There is something that I'm sure of,' enjoined Chase, 'if Guy Pender and Radcliffe have done their stuff, there should be a stack of boodle in my bank shortly. I have every intention of spending it.'

'You got away from Albertville just in time, but Op-Sud thought you might pitch up here,' said Morley, leading Chase to his jeep.

'What happens if they send a party up here to get me?'

'I'll have you out on patrol, only calling you in when it's safe,' answered Morley, starting the jeep's engine.

Morley drove into the courtyard at the back of Ops HQ. He saw Captain Pender poke his head around the door. Morley parked the jeep and turned to Chase in the passenger seat. 'You must be hungry after your trip, Brad.'

'Too right I am.'

'There should be some food in the mess. Go there and feed your face and then come to my room. I'll take the mailbag.'

Chase needed no further invitation. He walked from the jeep towards the officers' mess, leaving Morley alone with his thoughts. He watched Chase enter before he swung himself from the jeep and strode into the villa. Pender was staring moodily through the window when he came into the room.

'So, Op-Sud's radio message was right,' he said, studying the officers' mess from the window.

'Op-Sud was right about everything,' declared Morley, taking off his beret.

Pender thumped his fist on the windowsill, his face distorted with rage. 'What the hell is Brad playing at? That stupid act of his could easily jeopardise our plans. This is the last place we want Op-Sud sniffing around right now.'

'Calm yourself,' soothed Morley. 'I don't want Brad Chase to see how you feel. It'll only complicate things. We can get round this problem if we don't lose our heads. Now go across to the mess and be friendly with him. You can let him know he can sleep in the room next to mine.' Morley gave Pender the mailbag. 'Hand this to the sergeant in the orderly room on your way out. I've got some hard thinking to do.'

Word spread like wildfire that Chase had brought mail and the orderly room became a hive of industry as letters were rapidly sorted by willing hands. A mail parade was called and the post distributed. It was too early for Bream and Morgan to receive any letters, and they weren't among the disappointed ones who received nothing.

'The *Rachelle* should be calling in tomorrow,' announced the officer commanding the mail parade. 'She'll be arriving with the rest of the boys who didn't sail on the first trip. There might, be another batch of mail on board, so keep your fingers crossed.'

Marvin wasn't expecting any letters either then or the next day, since he had not written to anyone. The parade was dismissed, and he was about to drift away when Ford called him.

'Force Tiger is on guard duty tonight,' Ford told him. 'You're guard commander and I'm duty officer, so get the boys lined up at 17:45 hours for me to inspect them. Six volunteers will be on guard at the same time throughout, the night in four-hour shifts so you'll need eighteen men. Write their names on a list and pin it up on the board outside the guardroom.'

'Yes, sir,' said Marvin reluctantly.

'I haven't had a kit boy since losing Abedi a week ago,' went on Ford. 'Do me a favour and search around when you can spare the time today. I must get a replacement before the new arrivals land and start looking for slaves.'

'I'll keep my eyes open.'

Marvin went to his billet and wrote out a guard roster which he secured to the board in front of the guardroom. He had time on his hands before mounting the guard and he juggled with the idea of finding Ford a kit boy. His mind came down on the side of selfishness, reaching the conclusion that he would utilise the time with a refreshing swim. In the space of minutes Marvin had changed into his bathing trunks and was heading for the beach. He swam in the cool water and then joined Morgan and Bream on the floating jetty, where they lazed in the sun, watching a group of mercenaries dynamiting fish from the superstructure of the wrecked ship offshore.

'The Congo has a few consolations,' laughed Bream as he turned over to let the sun tan his back.

'Enjoy it while you can,' grinned Marvin. 'I've got you down for guard duty from 22:00 hours until 02:00 in the morning.'

'There's my luck,' grumbled Bream, his happy disposition vanishing.

'Stop scowling. Five other guys are on with you. Besides, you can crawl into bed at 02:00. There are worse watches, you know,' added Marvin.

'Big deal!'

Morgan winked at Marvin and, before Bream was aware of the situation, they had grabbed his arms and legs and thrown him into the water. He came up spluttering. 'Bloody sprog!' hooted Morgan.

The night guard mounted without drama and Marvin brought the men to attention. He marched up to Ford. 'Guard all present and ready for inspection, sir.'

'Thank you, Sergeant,' said Ford, returning Marvin's salute. He quickly inspected them and then spoke to Marvin again. 'Instruct them on their duties and dismiss the ones who aren't on the first watch.'

Ford retired from the scene shortly after Marvin began addressing the men.

'Just two points left now,' said Marvin in conclusion. 'As there are six of you on guard at a time, I want you to split up in pairs. One pair will patrol along the main street and another pair will patrol in the opposite direction. The third pair are to patrol up and down the beach track. When your four-hour stint is over you wake up the men who are on the next watch. Make sure you know where your successors are sleeping. Wake up the wrong blokes and you could be wearing a couple of black eyes by the morning.'

He dismissed the twelve men not on immediate duty and stayed long enough to see the volunteers on first watch sorting themselves into pairs. Satisfied that all was well, Marvin drifted off to the NCOs' mess. He stayed there until 22:00 hours when he supervised the changing of the guard. He watched them move off into the night, before going to bed.

Bream and Hamilton were chosen to patrol the track from the Ops HQ villa to the beach. They walked slowly; their rifles slung casually over their shoulders. Across from the officers' mess came sounds of merriment. A coarse laugh, louder than the others, reached their ears.

'That's old Brad Chase,' tendered Hamilton.

'I'd know that laugh anywhere.'

'You know him then?' queried Bream.

'Yes, from the Stanleyville days. I was his driver for a month. At times I didn't know if he was going to shoot me or the rebs.'

'Bollocks, man. You must be joking.'

'Strewth I'm not. He can get mad as a snake. Once I was driving him along a road near Stanleyville when we saw a native waving us down. We stopped and we found out the guy was carrying a load of eggs.'

'Eggs?'

'Yeah, chicken eggs. He wanted us to buy them. Chase looks at the eggs and asks him how much he wants for them. The guy tells Chase that the eggs are one hundred francs each. "What?" says Chase, bloody-minded like. The guy tells him again. To my surprise, Chase reckons he'll take the lot.

'The Congolese bloke hands over the eggs and Chase passes them to me to put on the back seat of the jeep. While I'm doing it this the guy sticks out his hand for money, but Chase pulls out his .45 instead and shoots him dead. Blam! Just like that.'

'Christ!' exclaimed Bream incredulously.

'Chase orders me to drive on and then he looks at me. "What a bloody cheek," he says, "one hundred francs for an egg!"' Hamilton paused and chuckled cynically. 'Do you know, if that guy had offered those eggs at twenty francs apiece, Brad Chase would have coughed up without a murmur, but at one hundred francs … ahuh.'

'Remind me never to go into the egg business.'

'Too right.'

The lights in Baraka flickered out one by one as the garrison settled down for the night. Bream and Hamilton continued their lonely patrol, plodding resolutely up and down the track. Hamilton stifled a yawn.

'Our stint must be nearly over,' he said.

Bream peered at the luminous dial of his watch. 'Sorry to disappoint you, but there's another hour to push.'

'Oh, hell,' sighed Hamilton. 'Let's get further down to the beach and have a quiet smoke.'

Bream was about to agree when an unmistakable sound of a shot rang out. Bream flinched.

'Where did that come from?' he said in alarm.

Hamilton quickly unslung his rifle. 'From Ops HQ unless my ears are playing me up. We'd better investigate – fast!'

They ran to the villa and rushed through the door into the orderly room. Bream yelped in pain as he blundered into a desk.

'Who's there?' thundered a voice.

Before he could reply they were caught in the beam of a powerful torchlight. Hamilton shielded his eyes.

'The guard,' he shouted.

The torch was lowered, and they saw that it was Morley who had hurled the question at them. He stood in the entrance of the room where Chase was sleeping.

'We heard a shot,' said Bream.

'So did I,' Morley declared. 'It woke me up.' His torch beam explored the orderly room. 'Nothing here, let's try Captain Chase's room. Unless he's in a drunken stupor, the shot should have woken him too.' A patter of running feet reached their ears from the courtyard. Morley levelled his torch at the doorway and the panting figure of Marvin stumbled in with two other guards.

He halted, blinking in the full glare of the torch. 'Are you the guard commander?' asked Morley. Voices could be heard outside the villa, but Morley ignored the distraction and kept the torchlight on Marvin and the two volunteers behind him.

'It's the Major asking,' prompted Hamilton, realising that Marvin hadn't recognised Morley.

'Yes, sir,' he said hurriedly. 'Apparently a shot came from this vicinity.'

'There was a shot, Sergeant, and we don't need half the camp to track it down. You can stay, but tell those men behind you to get, back on guard.'

'What's going on in here?'

Morley pivoted the torch and saw Ford coming through the front entrance. 'We're about to find out, Lieutenant,' rapped Morley irritably. 'We were on the point of checking Captain Chase's room when you barged in.'

'Sorry, sir,' muttered Ford.

'Now let's look into his room,' said Morley, swivelling the torch beam through the open door. 'If he didn't hear that shot, he's either very drunk…' Morley stopped in mid-sentence as he trained the torch on the stretcher in the far corner. The others crowded around the doorway and peered in.

'…or very dead,' grunted Ford, completing Morley' s sentence.

Bradley Chase lay spread eagled across his stretcher, absolutely motionless. The wall behind his head was splashed with blood and the concrete floor about his stretcher was a veritable crimson pool. The beam of Morley's torch picked out an object in the middle of the pool. He entered the room and extracted the object from the gore. It was Chase's

Colt .45. Morley gingerly held the gun in his left hand and shone the torch over Chase's body. 'Damned idiot,' he said quietly.

'What possessed him to do it?' said Ford, hardly believing his eyes.

'He was in deep trouble in Albertville. He must have drunk too much this evening. I thought he had, because he returned here in a pretty distressed state. I heard him mumbling to himself before I went to bed,' explained Morley. 'The rest speaks for itself.'

'Fantastic,' said Ford mechanically. 'Brad Chase of all men, committing suicide.'

'Well, it's happened. Find a truck and get him down to where the coffins are kept next to the sickbay. I believe there's a priest coming on the boat in the morning to see the villagers. He can conduct the funeral service.'

Morley watched Ford supervising the removal of the body before returning to his own room. He closed the door and locked it.

The *Rachelle* docked at 08:00 hours and the new contingent from Albertville filed off the ship. Morley met the Italian priest, on the beach. The priest agreed to conduct Chase's burial at 10:00 that morning.

The Baraka garrison, including the newly disembarked men, climbed on to the small convoy of lorries outside Ops HQ. There, they waited expectantly for the truck carrying Chase's body to arrive. Bream stood in the second to last truck with many of his comrades from Force Tiger. Through their bobbing heads he saw the truck with the coffin on board slowly travelling up the track from the beach. The coffin, draped with the Congolese flag, was flanked on each side by 5 Commando officers. The priest stood braced against the back of the cab; his head bowed in prayer. A young Congolese boy sat with his tiny legs hanging over the rear of the truck with a simple wooden cross in his hands.

When the truck joined the column, Morley gave the signal for the convoy to drive at walking pace towards the small cemetery which was situated near the village by the track leading to the ruined Roman Catholic Mission. Bream found the scene moving as they drove slowly through the village. The funeral route was lined with Congolese villagers, all with subdued faces and clutching pale yellow mimosa blossoms.

5 Commando dismounted from the trucks by the cemetery. The coffin was slid off the truck and onto the shoulders of the officers and borne to the side of a freshly dug grave. A firing party of six mercenaries lined themselves in a single rank at the foot of the grave. The priest read the

service in Latin and threw earth on the coffin after it was lowered into the grave. As Morley saluted, three volleys were fired over the grave in quick succession. As the echoes of the last volley faded in the distance the other 5 Commando officers went forward to salute the coffin. The brief ceremony over, everyone trooped back to the waiting trucks.

'I wonder what Chase did in Albertville?' said Bream, remembering Morley's words as he boarded a truck with Hamilton.

'Whatever he did, it wasn't like Chase to commit suicide over it.'

'Well, he did,' uttered Bream.

'How do you know?' said Hamilton from the corner of his mouth. 'You didn't see Chase actually take his own life.'

'Surely you're not insinuating that...'

'I ain't insinuating anything,' cut in Hamilton quietly. 'I'm just saying it's mighty peculiar. That's all.'

When the trucks arrived back at base, Morley left the convoy and went straight to the radio room.

'Radio Op-Sud that Captain Chase was buried this morning after taking his own life,' he said to SM Riley. 'Include in the signal that I want a helicopter up here to fly me to Albertville.'

'Any special time, sir?' enquired Riley.

'As soon as possible.' Morley made his exit from the radio room and met Pender as he was about to enter the villa. 'Just the man,' said Morley.

'For what?' Pender asked.

'I need an officer to take command of the navy now that Brad Chase is no longer with us. You're the man. I'll inform Op-Sud that you will be taking over as from now. You can go down to Albertville in the Swift which escorted the *Rachelle* in.'

The helicopter duly arrived and Morley was transported to Albertville Airport. Sergeant Brogan met him there and chauffeured him direct to Op-Sud. He arrived in time for the afternoon briefing.

'Glad to see you here,' said Cartier. 'We have a lot to discuss.'

Lagache leaned across to Morley as the Major sat down next to Radcliffe. 'Thank you for your signal concerning Captain Chase. It certainly made our lives a little easier.'

'No public trial, you mean,' replied Morley, pleased with Lagache's appreciative response. It also indicated that Cartier was of the same opinion, otherwise the Belgian would not have said it.

Cartier tapped the large map by him with his cane. The room fell silent as he began the briefing with details of government troop movements during the past twenty-four hours. Afterwards, the Colonel touched on the latest rebel activity and then turned to Morley.

'Now I wish to mention something of special interest regarding 5 Commando, I have the word of my supplies officer that enough rations and ammunition will be airfreighted here in the next three to four weeks, enough for 5 Commando's advance up the lakeside to Lukamba. Once this rebel stronghold falls, General Kimbiti won't be able to rely on the Tanzania-Lukamba route for arms. The same applies to the rebels further inland. The only remaining question being, Major, is when will you be ready to move against Lukamba?'

'The moment these stores arrive at Baraka,' answered Morley without hesitation. 'I intend clearing a few rebel-held villages near Baraka within this coming fortnight. When these are destroyed the rebels will be hard put to circle around and attack Baraka after we commence the lakeside offensive.'

'Excellent plan,' agreed Cartier. 'Make a good job in cleaning up those pockets of rebels. I have to garrison Baraka with ANC troops, and I can't vouch for the moral fibre of the Congolese soldier.'

'Who can?' said an American military adviser, exploding with laughter.

Morley smiled thinly. 'The rebel villages will be cleared, Colonel. You have my word on it.'

The briefing ended and Morley booked in at the Hotel du Lac for the night. After eight hours of uninterrupted sleep in his mosquito-proof room and a full breakfast under his belt, he flew back to Baraka by helicopter to plan the advance.

He called his officers together at Operational Headquarters and passed on the information he had received from Op-Sud. He unravelled a map and pointed a finger at two villages in close proximity to each other, just ten miles north up the coast road from Baraka.

'Lumona and Subuni,' he said distinctly. 'Both villages are one hundred per cent Simba and must be destroyed before we mount our offensive against Lukamba.' Morley glanced up from the map and eyed an officer sporting a bushy moustache. 'You, Captain Vivian, will combine Force Tiger with Force Leopard under your command for this operation. Both forces are to trek across the hills and hit the villages by sweeping lakeward once you're parallel with them.' Morley's steely eyes shifted to Vivian's right and fell on Lieutenant van Nunen, commander of Force Cheetah. 'You will take your force along the coast road, attacking the villages direct. All three forces are to coordinate closely, so that the attack will commence at, the same time, preferably at dawn.'

'When do we begin this operation?' asked van Nunen.

'A week from today. In the meantime, I want Force Wildcat to knock out that 12.7 once and for all. It bothers the ships calling here. More important, it's near the route which Leopard and Tiger will take on their way to Lumona and Subuni. I don't want that 12.7-gun crew giving our game away.'

Captain Heever agreed emphatically. 'I can't wait to see the back of that gun,' he said. 'What's more, if it fires on the ANC troops coming to take over Baraka, they'll refuse to land.'

'That's another reason why it must go,' stated Morley. He checked his watch and rolled up the map. 'Time for us to eat,' he said. 'We'll work out both operations in finer detail after lunch.'

Force Wildcat duly went out under the command of Heever and waited patiently in the area where the 12.7mm gun was last observed. Heever, from his vantage point overlooking the bay, studied the terrain through his binoculars as one of the navy's Swifts cruised lazily near the shore. He wondered whether the rebels would rise to the bait. If they did not, it meant a long arduous search among the many nooks and crannies along the adjacent ridges.

He was not disappointed. The 12.7 thudded into action somewhere down below and slightly to the left where Heever and his men lay hidden. He trained his binoculars towards the gunfire and his lips parted in elation. Grinning triumphantly, Heever turned to the mercenary crouching beside him.

'Tell the boys to follow me, Sergeant.'

The next moment Captain Heever had risen to his feet and was trotting down the rocky slope with his submachine gun clasped close to his chest.

Morley was seated in the signals room when Heever's voice crackled through. He listened intently as Riley took down the message. He beamed with pleasure as Riley laid down his pen. 'Five rebels killed and the 12.7 captured, eh! All we need now is to knock out Lumona and Subuni and we're ready for Lukamba.'

'I'm sure we can do that,' said Riley, sharing Morley's optimism. 'Do you want to reply to Captain Heever's signal?'

'Mm, yes. Let him know that there's a bottle of Vat 69 waiting for him in the mess.'

Leaving Riley to pass on his message, Morley returned to his room to study the latest intelligence reports on the two rebel villages.

Three days later, at first light, the men of Forces Tiger and Leopard assembled in the courtyard at the rear of Ops HQ ready for active duty. Ford, in company with Vivian, checked the men's weapons, and afterwards Vivian spoke to them.

'We shall be leaving camp in single file with a space of three yards between each man. No one is to walk on any footpaths unless it can't be helped. There's supposed to be about three hundred rebels in the two villages, and we number seventy, including the boys of Force Cheetah who are going up the coast road. I don't think that I have to impress upon you to keep noise to a minimum on the way there. Obviously, it will pay us to surprise them. Okay, shoulder your arms and let's move out quietly.'

The mercenaries walked from Baraka at an easy gait. They had a long hike ahead of them. Although the rebel villages were only ten miles away as the crow flies, the route they would be taking over the hills would double the distance. Sketchy maps of the area showed both villages nestling near the shore and a mile from a high ridge, that ran around and then down to them in the form of a crooked elbow. Both villages also straddled the coast road which 5 Commando would take on the advance in Lukamba. Morley's battle plan called for Forces Leopard and Tiger to bivouac along the high ridge overlooking the villages, in readiness for a dawn attack the next day.

With the morning sun warming their backs and Baraka behind them, the two forces comprising fifty men left the road and made their way through a bevy of derelict mud huts which had all but disappeared from view among the encroaching jungle. Shoulder-high grass spitefully welcomed them on the other side. The mercenaries waded through it, painfully aware of the sharp green blades cutting across their bare arms.

Bream followed the example of other mercenaries by rolling down his shirt sleeves to protect his arms. He was enjoying the patrol so far, but did not relish the thought of climbing the steep jungle-clad slopes that lay ahead. He was glad to note that he was not alone in his thoughts. The others were also casting jaundiced eyes towards the hostile landscape.

Vivian called a brief halt at midday and they rested in a line stretching up one of the hills, completely invisible from the outside world. The day's heat was telling on their bodies and water bottles were nearly empty by the time they moved up the hill again. Halfway through the afternoon they stopped at a small stream to eat a lunch of bully beef and biscuits and to refill their water bottles. The threat of contracting bilharzia was totally ignored as they drank straight from the stream after replenishing their meagre water supplies.

By late afternoon they had put the worst part of the journey behind them. Only one more hill stood between them and the long angular ridge where they would rest for the night, Ford took a compass bearing and then gazed at the crimson sun ebbing towards the horizon. He smiled tiredly at Vivian.

'If it's any consolation, we're on schedule,' he said pocketing the compass.

'I couldn't give a cuss how many rebs there are in those villages, I'm going to sleep good tonight,' grunted Vivian, heaving his pack further up his back.

'You carry on,' said Ford. 'I'll stay here for a while and watch out for lame ducks.' He studied each mercenary passing him. When Hamilton approached, Ford noticed that he was under considerable strain from carrying Force Leopard's machine-gun. 'Struggling?' he asked sympathetically.

Hamilton stopped and wiped his perspiring face with a shirt sleeve. 'I'd be a liar if I said I wasn't,' he wheezed.

'Let your number two give you a break,' suggested Ford.

Hamilton shook his head in stubborn defiance. 'Not a chance. I've got it this far and I'll bloody well lug it the rest of the way.'

'Do you know how Tiger's machine-gunner is making out?'

'About the same as me, I guess.'

'All right. Push on, but don't bust a gut.'

With that, Ford hurried up the line to join Vivian.

'Everything okay?' queried Vivian.

'As much as we can hope for.'

Vivian gritted his teeth as he started hiking up the lower slopes of the hill. 'I'm taking a nice long holiday after this contract,' he said to Ford, 'and it'll be in a place so flat you could see a cat blink at five miles.'

'You're lucky. My girlfriend wants to go to Switzerland for winter sports.'

'I suggest you pick a less sadistic girlfriend,' said Vivian.

They dragged their weary legs up the hill with the rest of the men strung out behind them. Ford reached the top a moment before Vivian and, to his surprise, he saw Ford crouch down quickly. Vivian immediately signalled the men behind him to stop.

'What have you seen?' he whispered, crawling up to Ford.

'Nothing – yet. But I'm sure I heard voices.'

Vivian licked one of his fingers and held it up in the air. 'You could be right. There's not much wind, but what there is is blowing in our direction.'

'And there they are,' uttered Ford in muted tones.

They watched with bated breath as they observed a small band of armed rebels ascending the same hill less than one hundred yards from their position.

'Twelve of them and coming our way,' murmured Vivian. 'Bang goes our surprise attack.'

'Don't let the buggers out of your sight. I'm going to get some men up here,' whispered Ford as he edged backwards.

'What's the flap?' asked Morgan when Ford slid down beside him.

'Rebels over the top. Get your rifle off safety and move very quietly up to Captain Vivian. Take Bream with you. Where's Hamilton?'

'Behind Bream, I think.'

'Okay, I'll find him. You two get up that slope quickly and quietly.' Ford parted the grass a few paces down the slope and found Hamilton sitting on his haunches, cradling his machine-gun. His mate sat next to him with a belt of bullets round his neck. 'Get that GPMG set up on top of this hill as fast as you can. There's a group of rebels coming straight for us, not that they know it.' He winced as Hamilton cocked the machine-gun with a pronounced click.

'Better to do it here than up there,' muttered Hamilton. He unfolded the bipod and got to his feet with his number two carefully holding the belt. Ford crept up the hill again with them stalking silently in his footsteps.

'Now, Harper,' said Hamilton, erecting the GPMG alongside Ford, 'Feed that belt in nice and easy so we don't get a jam.'

Harper, Hamilton's number two, assured him that he would. With that, Hamilton settled down behind the machine-gun, shoving the butt firmly into his right shoulder. Vivian, Ford, Morgan and Bream also raised their guns and brought them to bear on the unsuspecting rebels.

'Get ready,' whispered Vivian when the rebels had climbed to within forty yards of them. Their voices were quite audible, and Vivian could even see a flash of white teeth as one of them spoke. 'Right,' he said quickly. 'Blast 'em!'

Their combined shooting smashed the brittle silence. Hot, empty shells cascaded from the GPMG as Hamilton spewed bullets into the main body of rebels. Three rebels on the extreme left fell prey to Ford's submachine-gun, meanwhile Bream and Morgan concentrated on sniping at the ones who had survived Hamilton's initial burst. Two rebels fled down the hill towards a patch of thorn trees. Vivian sprang up and started hosing bullets after them. He saw one pitch forward, but the other rebel made good his escape. The shots died away. Vivian surveyed the carnage on the side of the hill.

'We stitched those over good,' he said jubilantly, 'But I'm really sorry about missing that one rebel.'

'It's not a calamity,' said Ford. 'Our firing has probably been heard in the villages. Let's go and see if any of them are still breathing.'

They found only two alive and these were quickly despatched with well-placed bullets. Ford collected the dead rebel's weapons and stripped out the vital parts which he threw into the bush. 'That's that,' he said, brushing his hands. 'What's our next, move?'

'I'll let you know in a minute,' said Vivian tramping up the hill. 'Where the hell are you hiding yourself, Ames?' he called from the top. Force Leopard's radio operator appeared from a patch of scrub. 'Get your PRCIO working. I want to contact base.'

Ames switched on the set and tuned it to the required frequency. He made contact with Baraka and handed the microphone to Vivian. 'Go ahead,' he said.

'Leopard to Queen. Stand by for message. Over.'

'Queen to Leopard,' came Riley's voice. 'Receiving you four-by-five. Send your message. Over.'

'Leopard to Queen. Made unavoidable, repeat, unavoidable contact with enemy. Eleven enemy killed. Our casualties nil. Element of surprise gone. Permission to attack villages today. Over.'

'Queen to Leopard. I read you clearly. Wait, five. I repeat, wait five. I am contacting Sunray. Over.'

'Roger and over.'

Vivian waited impatiently for Morley's answer. He noted the late afternoon shadows lengthening across the countryside. Every minute of daylight counted if they were to attack the villages before night closed in. Morley eventually came on the air to give his approval to Vivian's change of plan.

It was a ticklish decision to make. It meant attacking without Force Cheetah's assistance. Having half the distance to travel, Cheetah was not due to start out from Baraka until after dark. Vivian's men were tired too, yet he knew he must increase the pace if they were to arrive on target before nightfall. He handed back the microphone to Ames and went in search of Ford.

'We're attacking as soon as possible,' Vivian told him.

'Just as well. We'd lose too many good boys if we gave the rebs a whole night to dig in. He called to the men who had not taken part in the shooting. 'Time to move on again, so let's go!'

They filed over the hill and slithered down to the vale below with Vivian urging them on to greater effort. Ahead lay the last hill before the ridge. The mercenaries tackled it with misgivings, but were thankful to see that the hill sloped very gently on the other side where it fed into the ridge not far from the crest. They climbed up the path which ran along the ridge and, by mutual agreement, Ford and Vivian decided to let the men rest for five minutes.

During the short pause the two officers studied the rebel villages through binoculars. Both villages were less than half a mile from the base of the ridge and, through the binoculars, they observed the occupants scurrying between the mud houses like startled ants. Vivian switched his attention to the dying sun.

'Not much daylight left,' he said grimly.

'It's going to be bloody tight,' concurred Ford, lowering his binoculars. 'I vote we set up our mortar on this ridge and stonk them as we move down the ridge.'

'Not a bad idea. I'll arrange for it to be set up.' Vivian hurried off to the mortar team. He was soon back. 'All fixed up and now let's get the hell down this path to the bottom. I should say it's too well used by the rebs to be mined.'

'That's my feeling too.' A penetrating crack sounded, signifying that the mortar team had come into action. 'This is it,' Ford said.

Vivian jumped on to a flat rock and waved his submachine-gun towards their objective. 'On your feet, boys. We're going in.'

The mercenaries proceeded down the rocky path at, a steady trot. The thought of the impending battle made the adrenalin race through their veins, injecting them with renewed vigour. Hearts pounding violently, they ran down the ridge path at an ever-increasing pace.

The mortar fell silent when the mercenaries reached the flat grassy plain a few hundred yards from the villages. They spread out nervously in one slender line and moved forward towards the thatched-roofed huts in the distance.

Bream felt he was living a dream, as though his mind was strangely detached from the tense scene. The feeling was shattered when two shots scythed through the grass between him and Hamilton. He caught his breath on seeing tiny dark figures darting along the road in the middle of the two villages.

'By God!' shouted Vivian. 'They're running for it.'

He peeled off a quick burst and the rest of the men translated his shooting as the signal for everyone to fire. They stalked through the grass, firing from the hip. The dusk painted their forms in ghostly appearance, unnatural but lethal as they sprayed out a shield of fire to protect their quaking flesh.

The huts of the villages loomed steadily larger. As if by some unspoken command, the mercenaries broke into a spontaneous run. Bream was one of the first to reach the villages. He raced past a hut and collided heavily with a fleeing rebel. They hit the ground interlocked with each other. The pungent smell of the man's sweating body was almost overpowering as Bream grappled with him. He kicked himself free from Bream's grip and made a dash for freedom, only to run slap into a concentrated burst from Hamilton's machine-gun. The bullets punched him clean into the air. Blood showered from his lifeless body as he plunged to earth.

Bream sat up winded and reached for his fallen rifle. Hamilton had gone on ahead. Bream glimpsed his powerful figure vanishing behind a hut on the other side of the road. Using his rifle as a prop, he hauled himself up and staggered after Hamilton.

One moment there was dreadful commotion and in the next, mercenaries were milling around in complete control of the two villages. The only rebels left in the immediate vicinity were either dead or dying. The rest had beaten a hasty retreat to the north. The order was given to burn the villages to the ground. Huts began to blaze. Bream applied a bunch of burning reeds to a thatched hut. It roared up in his face. He moved away to the next hut.

With both villages consigned to the torch, the mercenaries started clustering in the road. They talked freely among themselves, joking occasionally as the tension of the attack wore off. They could feel the heat of the hungry flames on their bodies, and they watched one blazing roof after another collapse in a gigantic roar, spewing fiery sparks in all directions.

'Better than Guy Fawkes Day,' commended Vivian, tenderly fingering his singed moustache that had trapped a stray spark. He glanced to his left and saw a young mercenary proudly displaying an elephant's tusk.

'Nice bit of loot, eh?' he said to Vivian like a child showing his first good school report.

Vivian looked at him scornfully.

'You call that loot?' he asked in a derisive tone, his mind wistfully returning to the fall of Stanleyville. 'Man, you don't know the meaning of the word.' The youth wasn't in the least put out by Vivian's sarcasm.

'It'll still fetch a few quid in Jo'burg,' he retorted.

'I hope it does, because you've got to lug that overgrown toothpick ten miles down this road to Baraka.'

'I'll manage somehow,' he replied doubtfully, having forgotten the journey back to base.

'My arse you will,' guffawed Vivian.

Ford established radio contact with Baraka and gave a concise report of the situation. He signed off and went over to Vivian. 'We've played cowboys long enough,' he said. 'I think we should go now.'

'You're right, Ken. The party's over,' agreed Vivian.

After a quick count of heads to check that everyone was present, the force marched from the burning villages and down the unkempt coast road. Flames from the blazing huts licked up to the night sky, bathing the surroundings in an orange glow.

They arrived in Baraka tired but happy men. Hastily warmed up stew awaited them. They devoured it with ravenous appetites. Ford came through to the volunteers' canteen with a bundle of mail which had been delivered by a P-boat that afternoon.

'One for you Tully,' he said, flipping a letter on to a table where Tully sat with Bream and Hamilton.

Tully picked it up and glanced at the neat writing on the envelope. 'From my wife,' he said, inserting a knife edge beneath the gummed flap. A press cutting fluttered out as he opened the letter. He peeped briefly at the cutting before scanning through the pages of his wife's letter. Bream saw him frown.

'Bad news?'

'No, I wouldn't say that,' he remarked slowly, his attention now centred on the press cutting. 'Just puzzling.' Tully handed the cutting to Bream. 'What do you make of this? My missus took it from a Durban newspaper.'

Bream read it with mounting interest. He expelled a low whistle of sheer disbelief when he came to the end.

'Come on, Tim. Out with it,' urged Hamilton, his curiosity aroused. 'What does it say?'

'Well, according to this we lost six guys in our force during a night patrol. Read it yourself.' He passed the newspaper report to Hamilton.

'Apparently they walked into a booby-trapped hut, but names given just don't belong to Force Leopard,' enjoined Tully.

'I can't even recollect those names from among the other forces.'

'I don't suppose you can,' said Hamilton, returning the cutting to Tully. 'Ten to one they only existed on paper.'

'So what? It still doesn't make sense to me,' declared Bream.

'Nor me,' said Tully, scratching his head.

'Well, it does to me,' announced Hamilton. He pointed a finger at Bream. 'Do you know how much cash the Central Government pays out if you're killed up here?'

'Sure, I do. Fourteen thousand rand. It says so in our contracts.'

'And fourteen thousand multiplied by six?'

'Eighty-four thousand…' Bream paused and stared hard at Hamilton.

'But these guys aren't in the Congo,' pursued Tully.

'They are – on paper,' said Hamilton cryptically.

'So, someone is on the verge of collecting eighty-four thousand rand. Jesus, that's a lot of cabbage,' muttered Tully.

'Surely it would take more than one person to make this fiddle work?' reflected Bream.

'It probably did.' Hamilton studied his fingernails. 'Wonder if Brad Chase had a share in it?' he said quietly.

CHAPTER FOURTEEN

True to his word, Colonel Cartier shipped men and material to Baraka on receiving confirmation that 5 Commando was ready to march on Lukamba. The mercenaries watched the ANC troops with sardonic amusement as they came ashore. Almost every Congolese soldier disembarked with a wife or mistress. The women invariably bedecked with cooking pots or a crate of beer as she staggered ashore behind her man. Morley soon arranged for the Congolese contingent to be escorted to a makeshift barrack in the nearby village of Kontonka. The rations and ammunition which accompanied them for the offensive were taken by truck to a large bunker adjacent to Ops HQ.

The last supplies to be off-loaded was a consignment of plain wooden coffins. They came ashore balanced casually on the heads of Congolese labourers. The mercenaries cast morbid glances at the coffins as the labourers stacked them neatly next to the sickbay.

'Someone, somewhere, is expecting an awful lot of casualties from 5 Commando,' observed Bream as he watched the procession of coffins.

'Whoever it is, I hope we disappoint him,' said Morgan. He turned away from the macabre scene and strolled up to the NCOs' billet for an hour's siesta. He had little sleep the previous night, having been rudely kept awake by two once-domesticated cats who were quarrelling and had chosen his bedspace to settle their differences. To his chagrin, his siesta would have to wait. Marvin told him that Ford had requested their presence. Morgan gave a loud sigh of discontentment as he followed Marvin from the billet.

They found him chatting to Craven, the commander of Force Lion. Craven excused himself and Ford turned his attention to his two sergeants.

'The push to Lukamba starts in three days' time,' he told them. 'But the Major is sending us out tomorrow to Lumona and Subuni where we are to set up an advance base. While we're there, we're to rebuild a bridge which the rebels destroyed on the other side of the villages.'

'What are we going to rebuild it with?'

'We're taking along a truckload of planks for this purpose.'

'So, we're going by road to Lukamba?' prompted Marvin.

'As far as we can.'

'That's pretty dangerous, isn't it?' said Morgan. 'That road's a natural for ambushes.'

'Maybe, but fighting patrols will be sent out, along the hills overlooking the coast road. This should reduce the risk of the convoy running into ambushes.'

'It still seems dicey to me.'

'Everything about this beat-up country is dicey,' said Ford huffily. 'You've been in an ambush before, but you're still here. So, what's the gripe?'

'Precisely that. Ambushes aren't in the least bit funny.'

'Nor is reverting to volunteers' pay.'

Morgan relaxed and smiled. 'Okay, I get the message. You want us to get the boys packed and ready to go?'

'If you would. We leave Baraka at 09:00 hours tomorrow. See that we're issued with enough ammunition and three days' rations from stores.'

'You can rely on us,' promised Marvin.

The next day proved to be extremely hot, the temperature in the nineties with scarcely a trace of wind blowing inland from the lake. A Ferret car from Force Jumbo growled along the snaking coast road with half-a-dozen mercenaries braced around its turret. The remainder of Force Leopard sat on the heavily laden truck behind the Ferret car. More than once the truck was in danger of breaking a spring over the tortuous route. Somehow it survived the journey, and the tiny convoy rolled into the burnt-out villages. The mercenaries on the Ferret car jumped off and immediately fanned out among the charred huts in search of any rebel activity since the raid. They reported back that all was quiet.

The Ferret car driver reversed his vehicle within a yard of the truck's bonnet. The sergeant in the turret leaned over his .30 Browning machine-gun to speak to Ford. 'We're going up to the bridge to see what state it's in. While we are there, we'll carry out a recce by fire in case some rebs are hanging about the place.'

'That's okay by me.' The Ferret car drove off. Ford looked oddly at the scorched surroundings which had once been a thriving community. Morgan noticed the mercenary officer's dismal expression.

'Our raid was too much of a success,' he said, echoing Ford's thoughts.

'Yeah, and now we've got to rebuild a few huts to sleep in for the next couple of nights.'

'A spot of fresh air won't kill the boys.'

'Maybe not, but if the rebels have messed up that bridge like we've messed up their villages, none of us will have time to sleep.'

They heard the Ferret car rattle off a belt of ammunition somewhere up the road. Minutes later it appeared around a bend and drove up to Ford. The sergeant hoisted himself from the turret and jumped down.

'You're in luck,' he said. 'The iron stanchions are still in place and the gap is only ten yards wide. You should have enough planks on your truck to bridge it.'

'And no sign of rebels?'

'Not as yet, although they might send a few scouts along if they get wind of us. Let's face it, they'd love to know what we are doing back in this place.'

'We'll be ready for 'em. I'm putting a twenty-four-hour guard on that bridge and on our camp.'

'When shall we start rebuilding the bridge?' asked Morgan.

'Right now, before the rebs get too nosey.' He turned to the sergeant machine-gunner. 'Drive up to the bridge again and we'll follow you in the truck.'

Marvin and Morgan rounded up the men and the truck set out, after the Ferret car. A few hundred yards up the road they came across the Ferret car on a grassy hump with the sergeant dangling his legs in a carefree manner over the side of the turret. The truck drew alongside and stopped. Ford stepped from the cab and surveyed the wrecked bridge. The iron stanchions were still there, firmly embedded in the fast-moving stream as he had been told. He also saw that the stanchions still had iron girders riveted to them. In fact, all that was missing was the planking and that could easily be rectified.

'What do you think?' enquired the Ferret car sergeant.

'Better than I anticipated. Just a bit of sweat and we'll have that thing fixed.'

The force was organised and planks were soon being passed to men balanced precariously on the rusty iron girders. The bridge was completed before sundown and Ford personally drove the truck across to check that it was safe. He reversed the truck back over the bridge and climbed down from the cab.

'It'll hold all right,' he said to Morgan. 'Now get the boys to bivouac on this side. We'll forget about camping in the villages. The rebels might put in an appearance, so we'll have an ambush sentry throughout the night.'

Morgan approached Bream and Hamilton who were standing near the bridge.

'Set your GPMG up over there,' he told Hamilton, pointing to a patch of reeds. 'See that your arc of fire covers the bridge. If anything moves on the other side, shoot at it first and tell us afterwards. Tim will be your number two. I'll make sure that you both are relieved at 21:00 hours.' Hamilton went to fetch his machine-gun, and Morgan saw the Ferret car sergeant lounging against his vehicle. He decided to have a quick word with him. 'Where are you and your driver bedding down for the night?'

'Right here,' said the Ferret car sergeant, stamping the ground by his vehicle. 'I like being close to my peashooter.'

Marvin had meanwhile ensured that Force Leopard's mortar was deployed in a strategic position. Ford was impressed with its siting. 'That! s good,' he said. 'In fact, everything looks good. I was speaking to Baraka on the PRCIO a couple of minutes ago. Major Morley proposed to move out a day sooner, thanks to the speed we erected that bridge.'

'That's real nice. Incidentally, how far is Lukamba from here?'

'Seventy kilometres at a rough guess. How long it actually takes us to get there depends on the opposition we meet.' Ford stretched out his arms and yawned tiredly. 'Break out the rations and when the boys have eaten, tell them go get some shuteye while they've got a chance to sleep.'

Marvin distributed packs of American K-rations from the back of the truck. Afterwards the force settled down for the night. They awoke with a start at daybreak when rebels began sniping at them from a thickly wooded hill. The shooting was so erratic that nobody was in real danger of being hit. It was a nuisance all the same and Ford decided to retaliate with mortar fire. The rebels lost heart after the third mortar bomb had crashed into the hill and their sniping faded to nothing.

The afternoon heralded the arrival of Morley and 5 Commando with two Ferret cars leading the convoy of trucks and jeeps. The Major carefully inspected the bridgework with Captain Heever. Ford hovered near them and heard Morley's grudging approval.

'The bridge looks sound enough,' he said.

'I've tested it with our truck, sir,' interjected Ford. 'I'm sure it will take the whole convoy.'

'It had better.' He turned his back on Ford. 'Where's Lieutenant van Nunen?' he bellowed.

'Here, sir,' called van Nunen, running up.

'You've got exactly one hour to get your force on the heights. When you're up there progress along the hills to this village.' Morley pulled a map from his hip pocket and showed van Nunen a village ringed in pencil. 'Nungula, Lieutenant. It's about twelve kilometres from this bridge and there's a rebel roadblock just this side of it. I don't want to see it when my convoy gets there.' Morley refolded the map. 'On your way, Lieutenant,' he said briskly.

Van Nunen rounded up his men and they departed into the bush.

'Are we staying here for the night, sir?' enquired Ford.

'No' said Morley. 'We're moving on immediately to a Protestant mission six miles from here. That's where we'll be camping tonight.'

They reached the Protestant mission without incident. The building lacked furniture of any description and was very much in a state of decay, but it was sufficient for 5 Commando's brief stay. Sentries were posted and a field kitchen set up, after which Morley despatched a water detail to the lake with an armed escort.

The evening meal comprised tinned ham and beans, but the helpings were so small that many of the men were still hungry. Bream found two ripe pawpaw's which he shared with Morgan, Tully and Hamilton. Their appetites satiated, they prepared for sleep, knowing that Morley would make sure the convoy set out early next morning.

An hour before sunrise 5 Commando busily checked their kit for the day's journey. All petrol tanks were topped up from the forty-four-gallon drums carried on each truck. The machine-guns mounted over the truck caps were stripped down and reassembled to reduce the risk of blockages. The convoy got under way just as dawn was breaking.

The mercenaries could see thin pillars of smoke rising from Nungula village when they were still an hour's journey away. Van Nunen was there with his force to welcome them.

'We killed five rebels, and the rest took off at the high port,' he informed Morley. 'They seemed to have lost, the will to fight.'

'Unless I'm wrong, they'll make their real stand at Lukamba,' said Morley. 'Anyway, I intend chasing them there without, any respite. I don't aim to give those bastards a chance to stop and lay mines on this road.'

Van Nunen's force joined the convoy, and the column continued along the neglected coast road. The mercenaries passed through deserted villages, forded shallow rivers and braved quagmires of mud where the road had crumbled into the lake. On many occasions they saw signs that the rebels had inhabited places prior to their arrival, but it was only late in the day when they actively engaged the convoy. It occurred when the convoy had driven through a palm grove. The road ahead wound tightly around the base of a hill and the rebels fired on them with a bazooka, supported by small-arms fire. The shell exploded ten yards in front of the leading Ferret car.

The convoy halted amid a flurry of agitation as men leaped from the vehicles, rifles in hand. They crouched by the side of the road and fired back at the rebels on top of the hill. The machine-guns on the cab roofs of the trucks opened up, mingling with the noise from the Ferret car guns. The rebels turned and fled over the hill, leaving three dead in their wake. Morley promptly sent Vivian's force after them and the column continued its interrupted journey. Vivian returned with his men when the convoy stopped at dusk.

'We killed a couple before they scattered,' he said in a weary voice to Morley. 'You know, these rebs are really giving us a run for our money.'

Morley thrust a mug of hot tea in Vivian' s hands.

'You can expect a few more attacks like that, tomorrow,' said Morley. 'We're only thirty kilometres from Lukamba and they can feel us breathing down their necks.'

'And you hope to attack, Lukamba the day after tomorrow?'

'Hope? We damned well will! Big Daddy, three Swifts and two P-boats are sailing up the lake this very moment. They will commence bombarding Lukamba from 03:00 hours to dawn that day. I've a shrewd idea where the rebels will try to upset my plans tomorrow, but they're in for a surprise. I've already arranged for airstrikes on these places.'

'Ah, beautiful,' said Vivian, his mind at rest.

Colonel Cartier arrived at Op-Sud an hour earlier than usual, anxious to see what developments had occurred during the night. A Belgian adjutant-chef presented him with a dossier. Cartier thanked him. 'What's the latest news on 5 Commando?' he asked.

'Major Morley' s advance is proceeding to schedule and the B26 and T-28s have just carried out their first sorties of the day. 5 Commando broke camp two hours ago and the planes are strafing likely ambush points ahead of them. That's all the news up to now, sir.'

'And excellent news it is,' he said. 'Looks as though 5 Commando will be within striking distance of Lukamba by tonight.' The Colonel entered the briefing room and found Lagache gazing critically at the operations map. 'Relax a bit, Paul. I have every confidence that 5 Commando will take Lukamba. If not tomorrow, then the day after.'

'I'm not so interested in Lukamba as I am in Kimbiti,' declared Lagache. 'I have no doubt that Lukamba will be captured, but Kimbiti is a different matter.'

Cartier nodded sympathetically. 'Mental scars always take longer to heal. For your peace of mind I hope we get, him.'

'We must get him,' stated Lagache, his thoughts darkening with restrained anger. 'That man is made for a violent death.'

The Colonel produced a soft blue pencil and drew three arrows on the operations map. Lagache saw that one arrow was drawn in on the coast road south of Lukamba, another curved off the coast road through the contours of the hills and then into the rear of the town. The third arrow pointed straight at Lukamba from Lake Tanganyika. 'That, Paul, is Major Morley's battle plan. Kimbiti will be hard put to escape from that.'

'He can still escape up the road north of the town if Morley isn't careful.'

Cartier gave a quiet chuckle.

'He'll have a hot time if he does. The Cuban pilots are keeping a close watch on the road north of Lukamba during 5 Commando's attack. I can assure you that Kimbiti won't move far if he starts retreating in that direction.'

'It's a great pity we can't use napalm to burn away the jungle on that side of the town. There's a shedful of the bombs at the airport just laying idle.'

'You want me to incur the wrath of General Mobuto? He'd have the OAU down on his back in no time at all if we used napalm. They're giving him a rough time for using mercenaries as it is.' Cartier stared squarely into Lagache's face. 'You really are straining at the leash, aren't you?'

'If you mean that I would love to be in at the kill, you're absolutely right. Nothing would please me better.'

Cartier looked intently at the operations map and then towards Lagache. 'All right Paul, I'll give you the opportunity. Arrange for a helicopter to fly you up to 5 Commando's position this afternoon. I'll notify Major Morley by radio to expect you.'

'I'm most grateful, Colonel.'

'A word of warning, Paul,' he said sternly. 'Don't play the hero. I'm letting you go because your knowledge of the area might be of assistance to Major Morley. Please remember that.'

Cartier retired from the room, leaving Lagache alone with his thoughts.

Morley craned his neck skywards and watched Garrity's B26 fly towards a patch of jungle overshadowing the road. Puffs of white smoke streaked out behind the wings as Garrity fired a salvo of rockets. The foliage vibrated with sharp explosions and Morley fancied he heard someone cry out. There was no time to check as two ancient T-28s rumbled through the air over his head to shoot streams of tracer bullets into the smoking jungle.

The planes dipped their starboard wings and wheeled away over the lake. Morley sat back in the seat of his jeep and fanned his face with a small banana leaf. It was an hour past noon and his column had travelled to within ten kilometres of Lukamba. Taking into account the short halts to allow the planes to strafe suspected rebel positions, Morley felt that they had made good progress. He was not pleased, however, to learn that Lagache was joining them.

Heever had watched the air strike from the cooling shade of a palm tree. The engines of the aircraft grew faint as the Cuban pilots flew back to Albertville to refuel and replenish their ammunition. Heever stepped into the sun and walked jauntily over to Morley.

'I doubt whether anything could live through that barrage,' he said in a cheerful mood.

'Take a trip up there with a couple of men and check. You never know with these rebels. Some of them seem to have charmed lives.'

'Okay,' replied Heever, 'but I lay you ten to one that, we won't find one rebel alive.'

He called two members of his force across, and they trooped up the road. Vivian and van Nunen strolled along the sides of the parked vehicles to Morley.

'When do you want us to go into the hills, sir?' enquired Vivian.

Morley threw away the banana leaf which he had been using to fan himself and looked at his watch. 'In thirty minutes' time. Now are you quite positive of what you must do?'

'Yes, sir,' said van Nunen. 'We spread our forces along the rear of Lukamba and wait for Lion, Panther, Leopard and Jumbo to attack from the road. If any rebels run our way we shoot them down.'

'And don't forget that you must be in position before the navy opens up from the lake at 03:00 hours. You've got plenty of time to get there, so I shan't accept any excuses if you're late. Remember to transmit a situation report at hourly intervals.'

'We will,' promised van Nunen.

'Pass me your map board for a moment,' said Morley. Van Nunen let him have it and Morley showed both officers a cotton mill set back from the road. 'This mill is a fraction under three miles from Lukamba. Come what may, I tm taking the convoy there today. I'm making it our jumping off point for the actual attack.'

'You've got a fair distance to travel by tonight,' said Vivian 'With your permission, sir, I suggest that Lieutenant van Nunen and I get our forces together and start for the hills immediately. The sooner we're gone, the sooner you can move the convoy.'

'Perhaps you're right.'

The convoy rolled on again, leaving Vivian's and van Nunen's forces marching across the country. Morley allowed the column further along the road to pick up Captain Heever and his comrades. He noticed that they were guarding a dejected prisoner. Morley instructed his driver to draw up alongside them. 'Looks like I've won the bet,' he said.

''Fraid so,' answered Heever, pushing the captured rebel forward. 'We found him quaking in the grass. This might, interest you.'

He handed over a wallet.

Morley emptied the wallet into his lap and inspected a small pocket diary which was part of the wallet's contents.

'So, this guy's been trained in Bulgaria,' he murmured thumbing through the pages. He pocketed the diary and spoke to Heever. 'Bring him to me when we reach the cotton mill.'

The convoy continued to the cotton mill. Morley saw that double sentries were posted without delay before curiosity made him explore the interior of the mill. He discovered that the floor was ankle deep in crude cotton and crawling with insects. 'Probably snakes as well,' he said to himself.

He walked outside and supervised the placing of the yellow identification panel which would show the helicopter pilot, where to land. Highly satisfied, he lit a cigarette and watched Heever approaching, leading the captured rebel on a length of rope.

'Here he is sir. What do you want done with him?'

'Interrogate him.'

'Lieutenant Craven understands Swahili. He can help me with the interrogation. Anything you want us to find out in particular?'

'I do indeed,' said Morley. 'Some time back Op-Sud mentioned that gold is sent through Lukamba to pay for war supplies. See if he knows where the gold is kept when it's in the town.'

Heever's eyes lit up.

'That sounds like the proverbial sixty-four thousand dollar question.'

He yanked on the rope which was knotted around the prisoner's neck. 'Come on my old beauty. The quiz is about to start.'

Heever contacted Craven and they frog-marched the rebel around the side of the cotton mill. Morley's batman brewed up a pot of tea and Morley sipped it slowly, unperturbed by the harrowing screams coming from behind the cotton mill. Minutes later Lagache's helicopter droned into sight. Morley cursed silently as the helicopter honed-in on the yellow panel. At that moment Heever came up to him looking utterly defeated.

'It's no use, sir,' he growled. 'The bastard's adamant that no gold exists in Lukamba. He keeps on saying that the last shipment passed through three weeks ago. I hate to admit it, but I think he's telling us the truth. What now?'

'Give him a third eye before that chopper lands.'

A pistol shot rang out as Morley finished drinking his tea. The helicopter rattled overhead, hovered above the yellow panel and began descending. Morley went out, to meet it.

Lagache scrambled out of the cockpit, shook hands with the pilot and ran from beneath the rotating blades with his head bent. The helicopter rose up and whirled away over the trees.

Lagache smoothed down his ruffled hair with his hands and greeted Morley.

'Thanks for letting me join you.'

'I didn't have much option,' replied Morley in part jest. 'It seems that you know this area well, so you could be a useful man to have around.'

'That is one of the reasons for my presence here.'

Morley frowned. 'Why? Have your others?'

Lagache unbuttoned his shirt and Morley glimpsed the disfigured chest. 'This is just one of them.'

'Who the hell did that?'

'Louis Kimbiti. He did a lot more too.'

'I can well believe, but I doubt he'll do much more after tomorrow.'

He escorted Lagache to his tent where the 5 Commando officers were congregating for the pre-battle briefing.

CHAPTER FIFTEEN

The order came at precisely 02:45 hours. A crescent moon rode the night sky, imparting enough light for the mercenaries to move into battle formation. All vehicles except for the Ferret cars and two jeeps armed with GPMGs were left at the cotton mill under a skeleton guard. The drivers of the Ferret cars and jeeps spaced their vehicles ten yards apart on the road. The mercenaries, now in their respective forces, lined up on either side and waited for the navy's opening bombardment. It crashed out at 03:00 hours, the sound rolling up the calm waters to 5 Commando's ears.

The steady firing came as a pleasant assurance to Bream as he jogged along the road. He heard the rebel guns answering the navy's fire, but they lacked punch and were very sporadic. Lagache rode in the back of Morley's jeep, fingering the butt of his revolver. The distant shooting did not trouble him. He was going home and that was all that mattered.

The column reached the fringe of Lukamba in the grey light of dawn. The mercenary navy on the lake stopped firing. Their part of the operation now completed. The rebels attention had been sufficiently diverted, allowing 5 Commando to approach unmolested. The Ferret cars and jeeps increased speed and raced into the town, blazing at any target presenting itself. The men on foot trotted after them with their weapons primed for instant action.

Morley had given each force an objective in Lukamba which would have to be subjugated before the rebel stronghold could be considered captured. Force Leopard's objective was the post office.

Ford made his men keep their heads down as they crept along a low brick wall which gave them shelter from the rebels inside the post office. When Ford thought they were close enough, he peeped over the wall to gauge enemy resistance. The shooting flared noticeably, and bullets splashed against the brickwork as the defenders spotted him. He reeled back, his left-hand flashing to his face. Bream rushed up and steadied him.

'You, okay?'

Ford gingerly touched the cut on his forehead. 'It's all right,' he said. 'Think a bit of the brickwork clobbered me. Nothing to write home about.'

Morgan arrived by them, breathing heavily and clasping two rifle grenades. 'Give me covering fire as I launch these babies.'

He cocked the rifle and placed the butt hard against his right instep. As the rest of the force poked their weapons over the wall and fired at the building, Morgan angled his rifle and launched the grenade at the barred door facing him. The grenade landed on target, reducing the door to matchwood. His second grenade exploded on the corrugated iron roof.

Ignoring the blood trickling down his face, Ford shinned over the wall and darted towards the smoking entrance. He pulled a fragmentation grenade from his belt, extracted the pin and tossed it inside the post office. The subsequent blast lifted a portion of the roof and shattered every remaining pane of glass. Without more ado, Ford hopped into the building, shooting from the hip. His force rose up as one man, vaulted the low wall and scrambled after him.

Their sharp attack had the necessary effect. The few rebels who had escaped serious injury surrendered meekly, their morale and fighting spirit shattered. Ford's men hauled them from the building with scant ceremony. They were thrown to the ground and their hands tied behind their backs.

Morley set up his battle headquarters in Lukamba's police station which had ceased its civil function when the rebels first took control of the town. He kept in close contact with the air force as they flew over Lukamba. Garrity from his B26 radioed to him that the road to the north was sprinkled with rebels escaping from the battle zone. The Cuban added that the aircraft were engaging them. It was hardly necessary for Garrity to tell Morley. The Major could hear the noise of the B26's guns over his earphones. He slipped off the earphones and grinned at Lagache. 'It's just a matter of time,' he said. 'They're breaking up fast.'

The shooting finally decreased to isolated firing where pockets of resistance still held out. A smattering of shots were faintly heard from the heights above Lukamba when Vivian's and van Nunen's forces tackled the rebels fleeing in their direction. Both sides registered casualties, but the rebel dead and wounded far outweighed those of 5 Commando. Morley and Lagache held hurried identification parades of prisoners and also checked on the rebel corpses. Nowhere, to Lagache's dismay, did they find the self-styled general, Kimbiti.

'He could have skipped out the back way towards Tiger and Leopard,' suggested Morley, 'or else he's lying low in some building. I doubt very much that he'll risk going north with the air force buzzing around.'

'There's one thing I know for certain. Kimbiti's thinking like a cornered animal. He's desperate, but too wily to get trapped in a suicidal position.'

'What makes you so sure?'

'I've been following Kimbiti's fortunes too long, that's why.' Lagache lit a cigarette, his mind in turmoil. Nothing would shake the thinking that his quarry was close to hand. Hell, he could almost smell him. He threw away the cigarette and clicked his fingers in exasperation. 'I know he's around here. I know.' Suddenly Lagache's eyes widened. He darted a look at Morley. 'I bet the bastard's holing up in my plantation, hoping to escape later by boat.'

'That's quite a thought,' said Morley. 'Worth following up too. If you're keen enough, I'll assign some of my men to go with you in one of the jeeps. A radio operator can go along as well so that you can notify me immediately should you discover anything.'

Morley detailed Ford to escort the Belgian. Ford in turn chose Morgan, Bream, Hamilton, Tully and Ames to join him. Lagache, knowing the route, offered to drive. Ford readily agreed but sat next to Lagache with a GPMG mounted in front of him. The others, including Ames with his field set, squeezed into the back of the jeep.

'Is this plantation of yours far?' enquired Ford as they drove off.

'Within spitting distance,' assured Lagache, increasing speed. Carlos Garrity spotted them driving from Lukamba, he took his B26 lower, recognised the jeeps occupants as friendly, and left them to continue unmolested.

They saw plenty of evidence of the Simba Army's retreat. Mangled bodies lay everywhere, having fallen victim to the guns of the B26 and T-28s. Lagache kept his eyes on the road, only sparing the brief glance to his left as he drove near Kele village, a reminder of more pleasant times. Now the village looked forlorn and neglected. He noticed that some of the thatched roofs had caved in. Saddened, Lagache pressed harder on the accelerator to put Kele behind him.

The six mercenaries braced themselves as Lagache branched off the road and on to the track leading to his old home.

The slender palms lining the track held some remote semblance of a past order. The more Lagache saw of his plantation the more depressed he became.

'Are we nearly there?' asked Ford.

'At the end of this palm grove, not far now,' he said mechanically.

A winged insect flew into Ford's right eye. He blinked rapidly, releasing his grip of the machine-gun to rub his watering eye. It was a mistake. A figure leapt on to the narrow track in front of the jeep, clasping a submachine-gun.

'Look out!' screamed Lagache, swinging the wheel.

Ford forgot his eye and grabbed the GPMG. The mercenary officer fired a shade too late. Bream felt a sharp thump above his left elbow as the jeep tore off the track. Lagache managed to avoid the trunk of a palm tree before losing complete control of the vehicle. The jeep sprang forward, hit the remains of an irrigation ditch and overturned, spilling out its occupants. Peculiar silence descended on the aftermath, only interspersed by the occasional low moan.

Lagache sprawled on the ground with every ounce of breath knocked out of him. He gulped in air and staggered to his feet, his senses reeling. Ford, meanwhile, had extricated himself from the foul smelling irrigation ditch and gone to Tully's assistance, who was groping around on all fours with a bewildered look on his face. Not far from Lagache, Ames sat up and shook his head before staring at his right leg. Dark red stains were spreading fast, across his jungle-green trousers. Ames was still staring at his wounds when Lagache hurried to him to give him first aid.

Hamilton stumbled from a thicket which had broken his fall. He looked up the track to the still form of the rebel who had ambushed them. Ford limped past Hamilton with a pistol in his hand. Hamilton gently restrained him. 'You can put that away. Only the bastard's dead. I should say you got him square in the chest.'

Ford holstered his gun. He grimaced as pain radiated from the small of his back. He placed his fingers on the tender spot and worked his fingers into the flesh, trying to massage away the pain.

'He did a good job before I killed him,' announced Ford heavily. 'Go back to the jeep and help out. Some of the boys don't look so good.'

Hamilton left Ford surveying the track and returned to the overturned jeep. He squinted at the body draped lifelessly over the side of the jeep and took note of the exit wounds grouped high up the spine. Then his eye caught sight of Bream trying to prop himself up with his right arm. He looked appealingly at Hamilton.

'I think I'm hit,' he mumbled.

'You think? You are,' retorted Hamilton, seeing the blood coursing down Bream's left arm. He pulled out, a penknife and slit Bream's shirt sleeve.

'Have you seen Roy?' he asked as Hamilton staunched the flow of blood. 'Everybody seems to be here except, Roy.'

'He's behind you, but he didn't make it,' Hamilton replied softly.

Bream peered round and closed his eyes in horror. Hamilton helped him to his feet and supported him as Bream hobbled to the corpse jack-knifed across the jeep. His white face puckered when he reached out to touch his dead friend.

'Oh, God,' he whispered.

He turned away and vomited over the grass.

Lagache finished dressing Ames's wounds and sat him in the shade. He picked up the radio operator's fallen rifle and joined Ford on the track. They walked up to the dead rebel.

'One of Kimbiti's lieutenants,' Lagache said, recognising the corpse.

'So what?' said Ford hollowly. 'My boys aren't in any fit shape to continue. Half of them are hospital cases and one needs a box.'

Lagache gripped Ames's FN rifle and stared towards the rooftop of his old home which he could just see through the trees. He looked sideways at Ford. 'I'm too near to turn back now,' he said in a low voice. 'If Kimbiti's there, I'll find him. Yes, I'll find him all right.'

'It's your indaba, because if you run into trouble I can't help you. You realise that don't you?' added Ford rather sheepishly.

Lagache nodded his head. 'I realise of course. You cannot leave your wounded unattended, besides you must try to contact Major Morley and tell him what has happened. As you say, it's my indaba.'

'I didn't mean it quite like that.'

Lagache smiled briefly. 'But it is, Lieutenant, believe me, it is. Now go back there and worry about your men and try to get your field set working.'

'Okay but take it easy. Nobody is paying you danger money.'

'Nobody has to,' he replied simply.

He cocked the FN and started walking up the track.

His old house took on a more definite shape through the trees with each step. Lagache decided it was time to take stock of the situation. No use taking unnecessary chances, he told himself. He judged that the best course of action would be to circle around to the rear of his house. With that, Lagache darted off the track and into the neglected fields of coffee bushes. They hadn't felt the snip of a pruning-hook since Kimbiti drove him from the plantation and they had run wild, affording good cover. He crept stealthily around the house and into the yard where knee-high weeds grew in prolific numbers. He stopped, listening for the slightest sound with his rifle poised for action, but the house lay silent.

Lagache ran quickly to the back door, his nerves taut with suspense. He pushed the door ajar and his heart fluttered wildly when the door squeaked back on its rusty hinges. He flung himself flat up against the kitchen wall, trying to stifle his harsh breathing. The wall felt cold and clammy against his sweating back, but the expected shots did not materialise. Mustering his failing courage, Lagache crept to the lounge door and peeped into the room. The walls were stripped bare of ornaments and what furniture remained in the lounge was chipped and dirty. Lagache noticed in particular the floral-patterned settee where he and Marie used to sit in the evenings. It was so stained and torn that it was scarcely recognisable. He swallowed hard, blinked back a stray tear, and retreated from the silent house.

In the yard he collected his scattered thoughts and took a grip on his emotions. Kimbiti must be in the vicinity. Possibly alone as well, otherwise one of his lieutenants would not have pulled a one-man ambush if more expendable men were available. Lagache's only hope now – and Kimbiti's – was the boathouse.

He stalked along the leafy track to the boathouse. To his rear he heard the vibrant engines of Carlos Garrity's B26 as the fighter-bomber swept over the plantation. Lagache took full advantage of the distraction and broke into a run, hoping that the aircraft would drown any noise he made.

The track curved back on itself and Lagache glimpsed the lake. A P-boat cruised the waters to the south. The sight gave him fresh impetus and he moved faster, racing around the bend where the track straightened out before stopping short of the boathouse. Lagache's keenness was his undoing. His running feet touched off a hidden trip-mine. It exploded with terrifying efficiency. White-hot slivers of metal tore into his side, mashing his hip and kidneys. He crumpled up on the track, his face distorted in agony.

He coughed painfully and blood spilled from his mouth. A shot cracked out from the direction of the boathouse and struck the ground inches from Lagache's head. He saw the P-boat on the lake gather speed, its bows misted in flying spray. The crew had obviously heard or seen the explosion and were coming to investigate. Another shot tore up the earth in front of Lagache. He reached out a quivering hand to where his rifle lay. He grasped the weapon by its barrel and pulled it to him. Dirt spurted up by his left foot when his assailant in the boathouse fired for the third time.

Whoever was shooting at him must be in a highly excitable state he surmised. Any man with a comparatively cool head would have killed him with the first bullet. Lagache rolled behind a moss-covered tree stump as the fourth bullet zipped past him. More blood trickled from the corners of his mouth as he exerted his failing strength to prop the rifle on the tree stump. He hugged the butt and wrapped a finger around the trigger. The P-boat loomed up quite large as the craft sped towards the boathouse. Lagache saw a mercenary crouched behind the heavy calibre machine-gun in the bows. The mercenary fired and chunks of wood flew off the near corner of the boathouse. Suddenly the boathouse door crashed back, and someone ran out holding an SKS carbine.

'Kimbiti!' croaked Lagache.

The arrogant authority had gone from the man. He looked insignificant and frightened, but still dangerous. Lagache fired at him. He groaned when his shot missed, although it was close enough to make Kimbiti squeal in alarm. Lagache had no strength left to fire again and he watched helplessly as Kimbiti searched for an escape route. After some frantic dithering he chose a path along the bank of the lake.

'Hey! We've flushed someone out,' yelled the P-boat skipper.

'I'm not blind. I can see him too,' retorted the mercenary swinging the .50 Browning to bear on the scampering figure of Kimbiti.

'Then fire at him! He's getting away!'

Toby Ashton aimed low and a little in front of Kimbiti. He fired a long, concentrated burst. Kimbiti's legs flayed the air as the heavy bullets tore through him. Then his mutilated body thumped down the bank to splash into the water. Ashton laughed in exultation and turned to his skipper.

'There you are. I got him!'

'You got him,' whispered Lagache who had witnessed the drama from the shady track.

The pain in his body was not so intense now and he felt exceedingly tired. The salty taste of blood rose up in his throat again to fill his mouth. Lagache closed his eyes and rested his head against the mossy bark of the tree stump. Before his senses ebbed away, he thought that Marie touched his shoulder.

He would soon know.

CHAPTER SIXTEEN

Half drugged with morphine, Bream and Ames were flown out of Lukamba by helicopter and taken to Albertville. They stayed with other wounded men at a hospital high on a bluff overlooking the town with a splendid panoramic view of Lake Tanganyika. The hospital was badly understaffed and slowly falling apart from lack of basic repairs. A Belgian medical officer encased Ames's wounded leg in plaster and rebandaged Bream's arm before arranging their passage to Leopoldville in one of WIGMO's trusty Dakotas.

The air journey took most of the day and the aircraft touched down at Leopoldville Airport after dark. A 5 Commando liaison officer was waiting to meet them. He introduced himself and saw that Bream and Ames were comfortable in a battered ambulance which he drove into Leopoldville at a perilously high speed. Through the nearest tinted window, Bream saw that they were turning off the wide airport road and down a road called Avenue Victimes De La Rebellion. Shortly afterwards the ambulance decreased speed and swerved into a courtyard of what appeared to be a three-storey block of flats. Both mercenaries heard the cab door slam and seconds later the twin doors at the back of the ambulance swung open. They saw the liaison officer smiling at them.

'6 Commando in-transit camp,' he announced. 'This is where you two will be staying for a while.'

Ames struggled up from his stretcher.

'Hey!' he exclaimed. 'I thought we were going to a hospital.'

'So did I,' added Bream in vexation.

'The hospital, if you can call it that, is on the ground floor. You will see it in all its glory.' He disappeared through the nearest entrance and returned with four Congolese soldiers in fatigue uniform. They lifted Ames's stretcher from the ambulance and carried him inside, with Bream walking behind. The liaison officer pointed down a passageway. 'The ward is through that door at the far end.'

They walked along the passageway and the officer opened the door to let the stretcher bearers through with Ames. When Bream got to the door he saw a large L-shaped room with rows of iron beds, some with mosquito nets, lining the walls.

Every bed was occupied as far as Bream could judge and Ames was lowered to the floor on his stretcher in the middle of the ward. 'I don't think that bed is occupied, so grab it before someone else does,' murmured the officer, directing Bream to an empty bed which he had not seen.

'Your mate can sleep on his stretcher. He'll be okay until the MO arrives at eight in the morning. Now, do you need anything?'

'I'd like a smoke. My cigarettes ran out before leaving Albertville,' admitted Bream.

'Here, take these.' He thrust a pack of Belga Rouge into Bream's hand.

'Thanks.'

'Don't mention it. You'll smoke like crazy in here. There's precious little else to do. Well goodnight. I'll see you both in the morning.'

Bream undressed with difficulty and washed as best he could in the bathroom off the ward. Then he climbed into bed and stared morbidly at the grimy grey wall opposite until he fell asleep.

The din of fast-moving traffic on the road outside awoke him very early next morning. His arm was hurting him badly and he prayed that the MO would come on time. Ames was in a similar state. He complained to Bream that his wounded leg had kept him awake most of the night. Bream went upstairs where breakfast was served for the ones who could walk. A French youth from 6 Commando who had a fair knowledge of the English language cut up Bream's food for him. He explained that he was recovering from a paralysed shoulder and arm sustained in a rebel attack. He had been hit by – of all things – a poisoned arrow.

Fortunately, twentieth-century antibiotics saved him from a lingering and very painful death.

Bream finished his breakfast and returned to the ward. A belated breakfast was brought to the bedridden mercenaries just as the medical officer walked into his surgery. The 5 Commando liaison officer arrived a few minutes later and went into the surgery to have a word with the MO. The walking wounded queued at the door for treatment. Bream was about to join the line when the liaison officer poked his head around the door and called him in.

The medical officer unwrapped the bandages and examined the bullet wound. He dressed the wound again and gave Bream a shot of penicillin. Afterwards he wrote something on a printed form which he handed to the liaison officer.

'What's all that about?' Bream asked as the liaison officer escorted him from the surgery.

'You're being repatriated to South Africa. There's a Pan-Am flight leaving for the Republic tonight. I'll try to get you on it.'

'What about my mate? Is he coming with me?'

'The MO wants to keep Ames here for another day. Just a precaution, nothing more.'

Bream broke the news to Ames. He took it, well.

'You can set up the drinks in the Federal,' he said.

The rest of the day dragged for Bream as he waited for transportation to the airport. It finally arrived and, at midnight, the 5 Commando liaison officer said goodbye to him at the customs barrier. 'Have a good trip and look after that arm of yours.'

'I will,' promised Bream. He turned to go.

'Hang on a bit. I've just thought of something I want to ask you.'

'Oh?'

'Weren't you great buddies with Roy Morgan?'

'Yes, but who told you?'

'Ames did. Funnily enough I was in communication with Albertville today. His name cropped up in connection with a woman called Rita Viljoen.'

'The name doesn't ring a bell with me.'

'She's a widow. Her husband was killed up here on the last contract.'

'Okay. So she's a widow of a mercenary, but what has that to do with Roy?'

'Only that his will is made out in her favour. Just wondered whether you knew her.'

'No, and with her luck I don't want to.'

The liaison officer laughed. 'Nor me. She sounds like the original kiss of death. You'd better go now, or you'll miss that flight.'

Bream boarded the Pan-Am Boeing 707 and slipped into a seat next to a middle-aged American couple. A cheerful young airhostess strapped him in for take-off, giving him a warm smile as she did it. 'Looking forward to home?' she asked.

'Very much.'

'A few hours and you'll be there, so sit back and enjoy the flight.'

The airliner taxied from the bay and whispered down the runway. It turned at the end and Bream with the other passengers felt the engines building up for take-off. Suddenly they were racing along the runway, gaining speed every second. The airliner took off smoothly and soon the lights of Leopoldville Airport receded in the distance. The airliner steadily gained height and when it levelled out the air hostess came to help Bream loosen his seat belt. The tension in his body, accumulated through the previous months, gradually slackened with every minute of flying time. Suddenly he felt dreadfully tired and he shut his eyes, wishing that Roy Morgan was going home with him. A tap on his good arm made him look round. He discovered the American woman looking at him.

'Say,' she said, studying his jungle-green uniform and the sling mothering his wounded arm. 'Say, but aren't you one of them mercenaries?'

He gave a sleepy grunt.

'Do you fight in many countries?'

'No,' he said, hoping that his reply would terminate the conversation The woman still persisted.

'You've only fought in the Congo? Against communism?'

'Christ knows,' he said defeatedly, peering at her with heavy-lidded eyes.

'Oh,' she uttered.

Her husband leaned across and placed a reassuring hand on Bream's knee. 'Don't upset yourself,' he said sympathetically. 'I know exactly how you feel. Before the last war I took off for Spain and fought in the International Brigade. I wasn't the only young idealist for that matter.

Many of us went, some of us didn't make it back. Communism, fascism, patriotism or simply fighting for money. When you've seen it, been in it, and you're going home well, I just know how it is. Let me get you a drink.'

Bream looked out of the airliner as the woman's husband tried to attract an air hostess's attention. He saw the red glow emitting from the powerful jet engines. He yawned. Not long now, he thought. Just a few more hours.

'What would you like to drink, son?' enquired the American.

The air hostess hovered expectantly for the order, but no reply came.

Bream was asleep.

THE END